# The five principles of effective coaching

MONIQUE SCHOUTEN

# The Five Principles of Effective Coaching

## Meet your unconscious coach and step out of your comfort zone

The Dutch Library

# Contents

*This book is dedicated to my good friend Frank Strik. He proves that your circumstances do not define you; you can always decide how to deal with them. He is an example to many and a true artist of life.*

# 1 Introduction

## Always on target

"That's all for today." My coach stands up; our sixty minutes together have ended. I gather the wet tissues in my lap while he swiftly presents the paper bin. He has obviously done this before; the bin is already thickly lined with the sorrows of others. "Now thicker and more absorbent!" That's what it says on the box of Kleenex I am handed eagerly every time my eyes moisten. "Now, what is it that makes you feel this way?" is the question that usually follows. I put my tissues on top of the others in the bin.

I do not feel comfortable with this situation at all. I wonder if it's my own resistance to the therapy, my shame? Or is it his attitude? It's just a little bit too arrogant, the way he seems to assume the session must have been successful. After all, here are five teary tissues; proof he has pushed all the right buttons. I need to get out of here, as soon as possible.

"Thank you," I say while shaking his hand, mine still wet from the tissues. "Shall we make a new appointment right away?" He says, looking at me expectantly. "I'll call," I reply quickly, "the next few weeks are going to be crazy, I'm totally overbooked." He frowns. "Wouldn't it be wisest if you took an hour for yourself then? To help you sort out your thoughts? You wouldn't want to fall back into old habits..."

"Yes, you're right...," I think to myself, "...but not with you." An hour in the bathtub with some fancy aromatic oils, a good conversation with a friend, a brisk walk through the woods, even just an hour of staring into the fireplace: all this would be more helpful than another session of being subjected to this coach driving home the obvious.

This time, for example, I learnt that I shouldn't let myself be intimidated by others, and that I should learn to set boundaries. All true, of course, but I could have told myself that. A remark of that kind is nearly always a guaranteed hit, a scattergun approach, not a targeted shot. Every single person struggles to set his or her limits, to take their space, so aim in that general direction and you're always on target.

## Stating the obvious

The trouble starts the moment we are born. How much space am I allowed to take up? How much should I accommodate others? Will they let me out of the playpen if I cry louder, or will they ignore me instead? This does not stop as you become older; it just takes on new forms. Do you let others cut in line at the grocery store? Do *you* try to go first *yourself* when you are in a hurry? Do you share your negative emotions with others, or do you only show your sunny side? Do you keep listening, even when someone goes on for hours, or do you end the conversation? Space is an issue for everyone, an easy target for the scattergun approach.

My coach thought I looked restless. No kidding! I wonder how many people who are totally at ease visit a mental coach? Another easy shot, an open goal. He thought it would be better for me if I could learn to let go a bit. When I asked him what, exactly, he thought I should let go of, he had to pause. "More generally," he explained. "You come across as somewhat forced." "Interesting..." I thought.

Advice that targets clients' behaviour is often unclear and has only limited usefulness. What does the coach mean by "letting go" and "setting limits"? And more importantly, if you knew how, you probably would have done it by now. Something is stopping you from doing these things. That's what this book is about.

"But are we talking about me... or about him?" I suddenly wasn't sure. Actually, I started to wonder, what did he mean by forced? And for that matter, what did he mean by restless? I realised I had filled in his observations with my own interpretations of these words. But he probably meant something entirely different by them. I saw that there was no point in answering him; I didn't even know the question!

I am an obliging client, however, so I tried anyway: I told him I felt uncomfortable sitting there. I felt intimidated by him. Two additions to the growing pile of catchall phrases we seemed to be collecting. Brazen with frustration at all the nonsense I put his advice into practice there and then: I set my limits, took up my space and refused to be intimidated anymore. He didn't like it.

## Highly sensitive

"Transference," my coach stated. "A typical case of it. You are transferring anger onto me that is actually meant for someone from your past. It all makes sense, and you are allowed to; it's what you pay me for." "Yeah right," I thought, "whatever you say..." That man really had a knack for infuriating me, or was that transference as well? Meanwhile, he laboured on unconcerned, not once doubtful of his own analysis.

He could tell I was a very emotional person, very sensitive, by the way I responded. "Fierce, knee-jerk reactions," he stated, "do you recognise them in yourself?" No! I said fiercely, in a knee-jerk reaction... Perhaps I was highly sensitive, he said. It is more common than people think. He even wrote his dissertation on the subject. He said it was an underestimated problem in society, that highly sensitive people often feel misunderstood by others. I tried to get him to understand that that wasn't a problem for me at all, but he didn't seem to get it...

Despite all this he was able to push a few buttons here and there. Of course he was, I was at my wits' end! Just talking about myself for an hour brought forth many suppressed emotions. Expressing your more negative emotions does something to you. And if you take the scattergun approach to coaching, you always hit something!

## Dr. "hmmm... I see"

At least this guy had more nerve than my previous coach. He would just quietly murmur every once in a while to show he was still listening. He was of the school of thought that people themselves know their own needs best. The idea was that if you listen to your voice echo in your mind enough, the answers to your problems would just present themselves to you. He reminded me of a character from one of my favourite soap operas. It was a caricature of a psychiatrist, one where you go to sit on a divan and talk about yourself for an hour. The doctor just nods, mumbles, and writes in his notebook. Afterwards the client feels refreshed and is good to go. Unfortunately, you can do this just as well at home, in front of a mirror. It is definitely a lot cheaper. Or you could try it in the bar, after half a bottle of wine. Chances are there will be someone there who is equally inebriated to nod at your every word. If you are lucky they might even offer you another drink. A next round from you may buy at least another half hour of listening time. The next day all is blissfully forgotten.

## It's all in your mind

My very first coach ever was a warm-hearted, optimistic lady. She mainly explained to me that the key to happiness was in my own hands. "It's all in your mind!" She would exclaim cheerfully. The moment I learnt to think positively, my problems would just disappear. She was an expert at one-liners: "You are what you think!"

By coach I mean both life coaches and career coaches, as well as therapists, trainers and anyone else who professionally helps others with their emotional development.

Anthony Robbins also told me that, during a self-help conference. So did my countryman Emile Ratelband, "entertrainer" extraordinaire. With another Dutchman and management guru, Ben Tiggelaar, I learnt to "Dream, Dare, Do" in that order. All these men are right, of course, but how do you go about it? I dreamt, dared and did things all over the place; did I do them all wrong? The concept was clear to me: you have control over your own thoughts. You can take the reins in hand in life, and you have the power to influence much more than you think. It was practising these wisdoms, however, which proved a lot more difficult than I had imagined.

## Before you take up with your coach

What do you need to know before you set out to find a coach? What is the difference between a good coach and a bad one? How do you know if a coach is going to tell you the things any good friend can, or if he is a specialist who can give you real insight? This book teaches you to recognise a good coach. This is someone who helps you to understand the reasons why you can't seem to manage to change certain things about yourself, even though you really want to.

In order to change important aspects of your life you need self-knowledge. More specifically, you need an insight into your unconscious motivations and convictions. These are what block your personal growth. If you understand what motivates you, you understand what it is you do and why it is so hard for you to do otherwise. This knowledge is essential; it explains why you can't put your best intentions into practice. Your unconscious motivation is in the way, sabotaging every attempt at change. This is why it helps to make sure you understand it well, before you attempt to make changes. If you understand your unconscious motivation, you know when you are unconsciously digging in your heels. Intentions of self-improvement without this knowledge are like bringing sand to the beach. Tips and tricks for a better life,

> On a conscious level we might want to exercise more, live more healthily, be nicer to others or be more disciplined, but our unconscious selves are much stronger. Our unconscious worldview doesn't like change and will resist it, which is why good intentions often do not become a reality.

however well-meant, will not have a lasting effect. This is because unconsciously you resist any advice that does not fit your ingrained way of thinking, your worldview.

## The scattergun approach

You don't just let go of your unconscious convictions; you defend them with all you have. Without your awareness, your unconscious self is always active. It keeps you in your comfort zone; it keeps you from doing things that don't fit your worldview. Your unconscious motivation drives you 24/7.

If you want to break patterns in your life, to change things in a lasting way, then you must have insight into your unconscious motivation. This motivation decides whether or not take action, and so it decides which kind of advice will be useful to you. The type of advice that can make a difference in your life is the kind that fits your motivation, your personality.

A coach has unconscious motivations too, and it is important he realises this. If your coach doesn't know his unconscious worldview, he will inadvertently project it onto you. Perhaps your coach has issues with insecurity. Perhaps this means his challenge in life, so far, has been to learn to trust in himself more. Unconsciously, he will filter every insecure remark from you, his client. He knows how to help you with this, because he has so much experience with it. He will explain how to overcome your own insecurity, how you have to trust more in your own authority. That is what he, in turn, has learnt from his own coaches. Unfortunately, chances are you won't benefit much from this well-meant advice; you are most likely not made from the same mould as he.

> Coaching can only be effective if both the coach and client know their own unconscious motivations.

Imagine you naturally tend to trust in yourself rather than others, because that has always been the safest way for you to survive. Your challenge in life might be to allow some more influence from others. You might have to learn to recognise and accept your own uncertainty and doubt a bit more. If this is the case, the advice to trust in yourself more could be quite misplaced. After all, this is exactly what you have been doing all your life. Advice like that only serves to reinforce your unconscious convictions, which is why it is actually counterproductive.

In this book, the concept of unconscious motivations is explained in the form of 5 principles. The chapter "Principles" explains the importance of motivation-conscious coaching; it makes clear what a good coach needs to do to structurally improve his clients' lives. The things coaches definitely need to avoid are highlighted in the chapter "Coach Alert". First, however, we will dive deeper into the worlds of the nine personality types. When you become aware of your motivations, you can take real, lasting steps toward a better life. That's what we talk about in the last two chapters.

Are you unfamiliar with the nine personality types and their motivations? While reading you could flip to principle 5 for short descriptions of the types, their worldviews and self-images.

Happy reading!

# 2
# The five principles of conscious coaching

## The right pair of glasses on the wrong face

Let us first acknowledge that there are many great coaching techniques out there that definitely have the potential to help many people. The only caveat is that they need to be applied properly. Dental braces are beautiful devices, but they are wasted on people who already have perfect teeth. The braces are not at fault, the application is. Buying reading glasses for someone with perfect vision is a similar waste of money. Again, this is not a problem with the glasses, but with the application. Part of the art of coaching is applying the right techniques at the right times, with the right client.

Coaches and psychologists have many sound techniques at their disposal with many available applications. Techniques such as NLP, REBT, Transactional Analysis, and Gestalt therapy, the Enneagram, Hypnotherapy and Family Constellations can all be very effective and worthwhile. Likewise, it can be very useful to give someone an insight into his or her core qualities with Daniel Ofman's core quality Quadrant, and a spot of Belbin or MBTI can come in handy as well. However, it is very important for the coach to realise, per client, what the applicability of his techniques are and what he is hoping to achieve. In order to do that, he needs to first understand the diagnosis: to map his client's motivations.

## High five: a handful of principles for effective coaching!

Every person is unique. The things that work for you may not work for someone else. However different we are, we all have one thing in common: we are all driven by our unconscious motivation systems. These are convictions and ideal images that we chase after, without realising it, 24 hours a day, 7 days a week. They determine our thinking and our actions. Most of all, they dictate to us how to stay inside our comfort zone, how to keep from changing. Even if your conscious self wants to change more than anything, your unconscious self will try to stop you.

A coach that really wants to make a difference in the lives of others needs to help people to understand themselves. He needs to hand them self-knowledge. An insight into unconscious motivations and patterns is indispensable in this process. This is what helps people to understand what they are unconsciously striving for and what they are trying to avoid. It helps people see the lens that colours their world. It helps them realise what convictions are at the bottom of this, what these convictions have brought them, as well as what they cost. A good coach teaches his clients what they can do about their limiting convictions, the ones that cost more than they are worth. A coach that respects the following principles understands how people work; he understands what they need to break through patterns that bring more pain than pleasure.

**The five principles**

1. Our unconscious systems motivate us 24/7
2. The complaint is not the problem
3. Behind every problem there is a conviction
4. The adjustment of a conviction leads to lasting change
5. There are nine unconscious motivations

## PRINCIPLE 1
### OUR UNCONSCIOUS SYSTEMS MOTIVATE US 24/7

Almost everything we do is done unconsciously; we live on autopilot, without thinking about it. Research shows time and time again that our unconscious determines about 95 percent of our behaviour, so it is just as well to know it. Your unconscious motivations determine your personality, your character. You are born with them and they will not go away.

Day and night, without realising, you both strive for an ideal image and try to avoid its opposite. Doing this 24/7 takes a lot of energy. Since your unconscious dictates that everything has to be done a certain way, you have to always be on the lookout for anything that disturbs your ideal worldview. If you are unconsciously convinced life is all about being strong, then your unconscious will concern itself 24/7 with avoiding its greatest nightmare: weakness. If you are someone who unconsciously strives to maintain a positive and soothing atmosphere around him, then every kind of friction is a call to action. Friction, conflict and disturbance must be a recurring theme throughout your life; you probably are the first to see where the good atmosphere is threatened. This is because you would do anything to keep the peace, and avoid unrest. Your entire system is attuned to it. Why? Because your unconscious motivation tells you to. We program ourselves so that our whole lives, and all our choices, are driven by this motivation; our autopilot works overtime.

> We often understand better how our computers work than how we work ourselves, and most of us have no idea of what makes us tick. Without this knowledge we end up kind of doing whatever.

Your thoughts and actions are determined by your unconscious motivations. They determine how you interpret things, and what meaning you give to the world around you. Without this self-knowledge, most of what you do is done on the autopilot setting. Sometimes this ends well, but often that is more due to luck than judgement. Knowledge is power. When you know who you are and why you do the things you do, you can decide to do the things that are good for

When we understand why we do what we do and get to know our unconscious motivations, we are better able to make conscious decisions. We can learn to take over from our autopilots. Insight leads to perspective!

you. This kind of awareness gives you more control over your own life. That's not just a good feeling; it also means you can get more out of your life. You can truly become the best version of yourself. You just need to know what to do, and what to avoid doing.

Under principle 5, the nine systems of convictions and personality types are further explained. One of them describes your worldview, your personality; it explains what ideal image you strive for. It also sheds light on what you try to avoid more than anything in life, and what the price of that strategy is.

## Eye opener

Because our unconscious motivations are responsible for almost everything we do, it is often a huge eye opener to learn what they are. One of the most common responses we hear in our practice is, "If only I had known this earlier!"

When you start to see your unconscious motivations for what they are, you will see the lens through which you observe the world around you; you will see how you interpret things. You will realise, then, how your motivations are just a set of convictions about life, ones that you are always trying to prove true. Convictions are generalisations about the world, about reality. They are subjective by definition and they are inspired by your unconscious motivation. Convictions are what drive you. Without your realising, they hold the reins of your life. If right now the first thing on your mind is, "That's not how it works for me," there is a conviction behind that too. If you are convinced that life gives you back what you put in, then you will see proof of that everywhere. Are you convinced that people cannot be trusted? Then you will prove that conviction right. If you are convinced that things go wrong unless you do them yourself, then that will be what you experience. It is precisely because our convictions are so stubborn that it is essential to know them. And not just your own; it is just as important to be aware of the convictions of those around you. It means you can understand each other better; it prevents misunderstandings and miscommunications.

## Through a different lens

We can all watch the same film and experience it completely differently. We can grow up in the same family yet pick up completely different lessons from our parents. I, for example, clearly remember my father always telling us to choose "an education that can be combined with having a family". My sister, however, is absolutely positive he always told us, "If you are good at learning you have an obligation to make the most of it." My sister and I are different types; we have different motivations, and so we interpret things differently. I knew that I wanted children from an early age, and I was certain that they should never suffer from my own ambition. Now, in retrospect, I understand this was part of my own unconscious motivation. I now see how the fear of selling others short has been a major motivation throughout my life. Without a doubt my father must have, at some point, mentioned that it is handy for women to be able to combine work and family. But I am sure he must have said plenty of other things as well. I filtered this out because it fitted my worldview best. My sister picked up something else, something that fits her way of seeing the world. That's how it works!

> Our unconscious motivations determine how we interpret our lives, the way we were raised, for example. We filter for the things that fit our unconscious worldview.

## That's because of my childhood...

A few years ago I met with two different clients in the same day. The first was very modest, his voice was almost a whisper, and he took up very little space in my office. During our meeting he explained to me that this was because he was the youngest from a family of nine children. "You just learn to make yourself invisible," he explained. I in turn explained to him that he was a type 5; that was the reason he preferred to stay in the background.

That very same day I had another client who was nearly too big for the chair I offered him. He spoke loudly and gesticulated with enthusiasm. It was as if he wanted to underline every single word he said. Now and then he would clench his fist to further emphasise his words. "Well," he explained, "I am from a large family. Nine children, and I was the youngest. When you grow up like that you learn to take your space and stand up for yourself." I explained to him that he was a type 8, and that that was the reason he wanted to feel and show his strength. This did not have a lot to do with his place in the family.

It is not our circumstances that decide who we are; our motivations determine how we deal with those circumstances. If you know your unconscious motivations there is always a choice.

The circumstances may have been the same; the choices were different. Your interpretation is shaped by unconscious motivations. That means that in the same situation, a type 5 person will draw completely different conclusions from a type 8, a type 4 or type 7. How you interpret things is more interesting than the facts of what you have been through. This should come as a relief; it means you usually do not have to change much about your surroundings. What you need to focus on is the way you deal with them. Your way of interpreting events is a part of you, is born from your motivations. When you begin to understand that, you will start to see patterns. Then you will start to see why you keep drawing the same conclusions, why you keep working towards the same ending. This way you can learn to take charge of your own future more. In the end we all want to be in control of our own lives, if only because that makes up happier. Being a slave to your unconscious motivations is exhausting and rarely satisfying.

## Fasten your seatbelt: the autopilot in action!

How do you avoid ending up with a REBT therapist when you really need something else? How do you make sure you don't work with a psychotherapist three times a week for a year, only to discover it didn't help one bit? How do you know you are talking to the right coach or therapist? How does a company know which kind of training works best for its employees? And which leadership programme is most effective for you? In other words, what will do you the most good? With lasting effects please!

The answer is simple: always first look for your unconscious motivations, the psychological DNA that governs all your actions. That's how you achieve self-insight. You start to notice how your autopilot is in charge of almost everything you do. It is behind the wheel 24/7, and with every kind of turbulence it warns, "Fasten your seatbelt! Stay where you are and do not move!" It is the automatic, and human, response to every change. This response is a reflex, we don't even realise we're doing it.

However sound the advice from a coach or therapist, there is always something stronger: your unconscious motivations. Your conscious self might hear the advice and decide that it would be wise to follow it, but your unconscious self makes sure that you go back to old patterns as quickly as possible. Without knowing it, you are led by your unconscious motivations 24/7. They order you to stick with what you know; they prevent you from making real change and from stepping outside your comfort zone. That's how they make sure you keep doing what you're good at, even if it bothers you, and even if those around you find it harder and harder to deal with you. We don't know any better and so we can't do better, as long as we don't know what really drives us.

> Our unconscious motivations lead us 24/7. So it's best to know what they are. If you don't know them, then they rule. If you do, then you are in charge. Insight leads to perspective!

Because your unconscious motivations are always active, and because they regulate everything you do, it is vital to know what they are. Otherwise you just start repeating yourself, and instead of living your life, you will start just surviving.

The paradox is that most of us don't know our motivations, and so we tend to run around like chickens with our heads cut off. That's why we keep spending so much money on books about self-insight, why we try new forms of coaching, invest in expensive training, engage in mindfulness and yoga, meditate until we drop dead, and why we are still not happy. The reason is that we still don't realise that something else is stronger than our conscious will: our unconscious motivation, the autopilot! It makes us quickly pick up old patterns; they ultimately feel safest and most comfortable.

> The first step in coaching, training or therapy should be to find out the unconscious motivations and convictions of the client. Only then can the coaching begin.

## Team scan: more insight, more cooperation

Team scans are always a bit of a party. During a scan, every member of a team finds out his or her motivation. Suddenly, people understand why they do what they do. What their qualities and pitfalls are. They also understand their colleagues better! "So that's why it's difficult for you to stand up for yourself," one colleague says to another. "You're afraid of strong reactions." "Yes," his colleague answers, "exactly, and now I understand why you have opinions about everything. You like clarity and like to take a stand, it gives you structure." You become less critical towards others, when you understand them.

After a team scan people respect each other more, and they understand what the other person's challenges are, what others still have to learn. Not because we want people to have completely new ideals, but because it just feels better when you're balanced. It feels good to be in charge of your own behaviour, not just a victim of your motivations. Self-knowledge, and more specifically, knowledge of your motivations, pays off instantly. Understanding your own behaviour gives so much peace and freedom. Insight into others also prevents a lot of miscommunication and irritation. People with self-knowledge are easier to give feedback to, because they know their own upsides and downsides. That's an added benefit.

Managers often tell us that their people are much easier to direct after a team scan, because they are much more open to feedback. They recognise feedback better because they know themselves and they know what they have to learn. This leads people to take more responsibility for their own behaviour, to point fingers less. They are easier to manage and coach. Knowledge of unconscious motivations also increases your personal efficacy, ultimately benefiting the whole team.

When you discover your unconscious motivations, you also learn what your core qualities are. You will then see what you need to learn to get the most from yourself and your relationships. You learn what you need from your employer or co-workers, but also what it is you can offer them. This improves cooperation drastically. It also has a tremendously positive influence on the working atmosphere, which in turn benefits performance. Team scans are recommended for any team.

## Scan your motivations

Not only in teams, but everywhere where at least two people come together, patterns are created. Sometimes it's difficult to see what problems or behaviour came from whom. If you know your own motivations, and those of the other, it becomes crystal clear who owns what behaviour in a relationship. It makes communication nearly effortless; it instantly improves the relationship.

> If you know your unconscious motivations, you understand your own history and choices better. This realisation can stop you from becoming a scratched record, from repeating yourself.

The minute people discover their unconscious motivations, it is as if they can suddenly see clearly. Suddenly they understand the origins of their behaviour. They can retroactively contextualise certain choices in their lives. This also means they can avoid making the same mistakes in the future. How that works exactly is explained later in this book.

It's always heart-warming to see what happens when people realise what their unconscious motivation is. It provides one insight after the other. "So that's why I always think things have to be done my way," or, "That's why I'm convinced they're going to find out I'm not that good after all." Now I understand why I treat my own needs as unimportant," or, "That's why I always behave a little bit differently from everyone else." "Now I understand why I always need to know everything," or, "That's why I run away from the difficult things in life." Recognition gives you a lot of insight into yourself, and makes you understand a lot better why you do what you do. The opposite is also true: when we do not know our unconscious motivations, we actually kind of do whatever. We keep making the same mistakes over and over again.

## Conclusion

Your unconscious motivations drive you 24/7. They also determine how you interpret things, what meaning you assign to them. They explain why you make certain choices. Every coach, manager and educator should understand why an insight into motivations is so important. Likewise, if you want to understand yourself better, if you want to help yourself move forward, knowing your own motivations is an absolute must. Only then will you discover the ideal you're chasing after, what you most of all want to avoid, and how you end up frustrating yourself and those around you. This self-knowledge is very useful; it gives you influence. All of a sudden you understand why you always go for the same type of man, why you unconsciously work your way towards rejection, and what you can do to break the vicious cycle you are unwittingly trapped in. That's alasting improvement!

Just discovering their unconscious motivations alone has a great effect on people. From that moment onward they see clearly what they do unconsciously and what the effects are of that behaviour, both positive and negative. That gives you freedom of choice. You can keep doing what you're used to, with familiar results, or you can choose an alternative. This may sound simple, and in a way, it is. The only provision is that you can only choose alternative behaviour if you let go of an old conviction. That, my friend, may take a bit of effort. I will explain more about that under principle 4.

## PRINCIPLE 2
### THE COMPLAINT IS NOT THE PROBLEM

Principle 1 showed how nearly all our behaviour comes from our unconscious motivations. These motivations are the ideals we chase after, but that often prove unattainable in real life. This frustrates us. Most of our problems are frustrated ideal images in disguise. Even when we are confronted with a serious illness, or the death of a loved one, or when we are made redundant at work. However serious the problem is, it comes from a frustrated ideal picture. We want to be healthy, we don't want to say goodbye to those we love, and we want to decide when to change jobs for ourselves. Unfortunately life is tough and reality often deviates from the ideal image we have in our minds. We don't like it when that happens; it's often difficult for us to accept reality as it is. Our ideal worldview stands in the way.

When reality deviates from our ideals by too much, and if we are unable to solve our problems ourselves, we sometimes try to solve them by seeing a coach. We feel frustrated because our idea of what life should be like differs from how it really is. Perhaps you thought your marriage was sound, but it turned out your wife had been having an affair with the neighbour for the past three years. You have dedicated years of your life to your job but now your colleague was given the position you've been aiming for all that time. You feel like you're stuck in a rut, when all you want is an exciting, fulfilling life. You feel undervalued when you need to be appreciated. Whatever it is, reality is not like your ideal (read convictions), and this is frustrating.

People come into action when reality deviates from their ideal image. This bothers them and they want to change it. Problems are nothing more than frustrated ideal images.

### Changing reality

Most of the time, we try to find the solution for our frustrated ideals outside ourselves, and many coaches take up the challenge with zeal.

Something, or someone, around you needs to change in order to solve your problem. Your employer needs to be honest with you, your partner needs to be more patient, and your father needs to be more thoughtful. It's a shame things aren't that simple! It's not that easy to change reality and even if you do succeed at changing your partner, finding a new job or finally following your dream of opening a B&B in France, you haven't necessarily solved your problem. That's because we bring ourselves, our motivation and convictions, along into the new situation.

> When we don't like the hand reality has dealt us, we often try to change it; we try to make it fit our ideal better. We change jobs, find a new partner, get a facelift or try to lose weight.

Practice has taught us that, as long as we don't understand our unconscious motivations, we will organise the same patterns and problems in our next relationship or job. Even though you finally reached your goal weight, it doesn't mean that you can finally be happy with your body. Like I said before, it isn't your circumstances that define you, it's the way you deal with them. And your way of dealing with them comes directly from your unconscious motivation. Some people get more stressed out on holidays than at work. Some people feel rejected and crestfallen if their partner of ten years breaks off the relationship; others feel relieved. Certain things, like abuse, almost always lead to issues later in life. But in my practice I continually see people who deal with it completely differently, whose issues are completely different. Some victims of child abuse end up abusing their own children later in life. Others become the most kind and loving parents imaginable. There is no single response to any event. How you interpret things depends entirely on your built-in operating system.

> Reality is difficult to change. It is much easier to decide how we deal with our environment, our setbacks and ourselves. But in order to do that, you need insight into yourself.

## Adjusting our ideal image

Under principles 3 and 4 I discuss how a coach can truly help someone solve his or her problems in a structural way. Yes, now and then it can be necessary to change something about reality. Sometimes it really is best to change partners, to find a new job or a larger home. And it's wise to do anything you can to overcome illness, or to get away from dangerous situations. We all want to survive, but life should be enjoyed as well.

It is a challenge to recognise whether something around you needs changing at all. The majority of the time, thankfully, it already helps to understand your own unconscious expectations and ideals. It lightens your load tremendously to know which ideals are actually achievable and which ones are not. It helps you know when to cut your losses (without becoming indifferent) and when you need to push on through. You can identify the situations you can influence, and the ones you can't. That's what this is about, because then you can make the choices that are good for you. For the rest of your life, because the beauty of self-insight is that it only ever grows. You only learn to understand yourself better, not less, and you start to see earlier and earlier when you are working towards a goal that can never be met. This grounds you, brings you more in touch with reality; it saves you a lot of frustration, time and negative energy. It creates peace and balance.

A good coach looks for the ideal images that keep a complaint alive. That's how you find the real problem.

For that reason, a good coach always finds the ideals behind a complaint; the client's idea of how it should have been. That's where the real problem is. Your ideals come directly from your unconscious motivations, so all the better for you to know them well.

## Behaviour is interchangeable

There are nine basic motivations, neatly listed under principle 5. One of those describes why you do what you do, what motivates you and keeps you going. It is very important to realise that people with the same basic motivation can behave completely differently. Conversely, two people with different motivations may display identical behaviour. In other words, your behaviour doesn't tell us much about your motivation. That's why it's so hard to find someone's true unconscious motivation. In a way, a coach has to "see through" behaviour to find the client's convictions, their unconscious motivation behind their behaviour. Not every coach knows about the nine motivations, but every coach is capable of finding convictions behind behaviour. It's a good start; our convictions say everything about our motivation.

Behaviour is interchangeable; motivations are not. Two people might both be equally sensitive to the opinions of others, but for wildly different reasons. The reasons are born from their unconscious motivations.

Perhaps you can see that we behave similarly, always pleasing others, but don't be deceived. Perhaps I behave that way because I always want others to think of myself as good company, and you could be unconsciously trying to avoid conflict by keeping a peaceful atmosphere. The behaviour is the same; the motivation is different. That's why a coach should never be distracted by the complaint his client has. Complaints deal with behaviour and everyone can behave the same way. Everyone can be bothered by his or her own procrastination, everyone can be afraid of conflict.

We all feel like we end up empty-handed now and then, like we're invisible, or undervalued. We can all feel pain when we lose a loved one or when illness threatens our quality of life. We are all familiar with feeling overly responsible for others, feeling like we don't have enough time for ourselves, that we are selling ourselves short. None of us are strangers to any human emotion. They are complaints that don't tell us anything about the story behind them: the problem. The reason that you procrastinate, feel heartbroken, easily feel rejected, that reason is what's interesting. That's what tells us about your unconscious motivations and about the real problem behind your complaint. A good coach always looks for the problem behind the complaint.

## Fighting symptoms

Stomach pains can have multiple causes. If the pain is so bad that you decide to see a doctor, he will ask you a series of questions. "How long has it been bothering you?" "Do you have a fever?" "Is it higher or lower on your abdomen?" "To the left or right?" "Does it hurt when I do this?" "And here?" And then the most difficult one to answer: "What kind of pain are you feeling? Throbbing, nagging, piercing, dull?" If your doctor can't figure out what ails you right away he can do an ultrasound or order help from a specialist. After all, he can't treat you without a proper diagnosis.

When I looked up abdominal pain on a reputable online medical service the following little phrase stood out to me:

NB. Treatment strongly depends on the cause, nature and severity of the pain.

Treatment strongly depends on the cause, nature and severity of the pain. If only coaches worked this meticulously. Finding the cause of the problem, it doesn't seem like a superfluous step but it is often disregarded. Much coaching concerns itself more with fighting symptoms than with curing ailments. A hot water bottle and some pain killers. The pain might go away for a bit, but if you're unlucky it comes back with a vengeance, and all the while the problem only grows.

## The complaint is not the problem

Many coaches, with the best of intentions, give mainly behavioural advice. This is because they are unaware of their clients' unconscious motivations. Sometimes this helps a bit at first. The advice makes you feel more peaceful and in control because you understand what you need to do now. Just take better care of yourself, just set your limits, let go a bit, and communicate more. With the one-liners still buzzing in your ears, you set out to make some serious changes for the better.

Unfortunately, once you get home, it isn't all that easy. "Let's organise more together time," you cheerfully suggest to your partner, intending to improve your relationship. She looks at you surprised, "Yeah right," she says. "You go see your coach and now suddenly you have the time to do stuff together? I've been begging you for years to make time for me; I guess his opinions matter more to you than mine. Well, forget it. If you want more time together, just start working a bit less." Yes, that's how it works when somebody starts moving things around; it creates turbulence! The other person will try their hardest to restore the balance. They dig in their heels and kick the ball back into your court. They unconsciously try to keep the old pattern intact, even when it's unhealthy and unsatisfying, leaving you empty-handed. But you won't give up that easily! You decide to cut back on your hours at work. Your employer is not amused. He had great plans with you and thinks this is a stupid choice. "This will have consequences," he explains passive-aggressively. Another kick to your self-confidence, but you push on through. At home you share the exciting news that you have finally started working fewer hours. "Have you gone completely mad? I thought that this year we could go on that big trip we've been talking about. How are we supposed to afford that if you work less?"

> Behavioural coaching is usually the same as fighting symptoms of an illness, rather than its cause. It rarely solves the real problem, and only serves to increase the frustration. It often exacerbates the issue too.

Anyway, long story short, coaching often results in a frustrated partner and a frustrated employer, not to mention you. What happened to all that clarity? What was the right thing to do again? Better go back to see your coach.

## Complaint: I keep putting myself last

Multiple people may have similar complaints, but the stories behind them can vary wildly. Those stories are the interesting part; they give information about the actual problem behind the complaint.

One of the most common complaints in my practice, for example, is that clients feel like they are continually putting others before themselves. Only recently I met with a kind lady in her early forties who complained about how little time for herself she was left with at the end of the week. Her children were fairly demanding, and of course a mother tends to put herself last, so her own needs often fell by the wayside. I asked her what she meant when she said she "puts herself last", what does that mean exactly? "Well," she continued, "like when I finally go on a girls' weekend away with my friends, I end up coming back Sunday night instead of Monday. That's because the kids have school in the morning and it's just better if I prepare their lunches; my husband always makes such a mess of them. He hates doing the lunchboxes and packing their bags; it stresses him out. Oh he'll do it, but don't ask me how! So I end up with a messy kitchen, unhappy kids, and a stressed out husband, even when I always try so hard to make everybody happy. My childfree friends always stay at the resort until Monday, and it's just such a shame I never can." "Oh well," I say, "everything has its price." She looks at me questioningly. "Apparently you get just that bit more out of going home than you do out of staying?"

## Psychological investment

Nearly everything we do is first unconsciously weighed up. When push comes to shove, we always pick the behaviour that gives us the most satisfaction. More specifically, we choose the behaviour that satisfies our unconscious motivation the most, the behaviour that keeps us in our comfort zone. The lady in question found out that she also benefited from her early abandonment of the girls' weekend. That was how she prevented causing too much friction in her family at home, because that would be the last thing she wanted! Neither did she want to miss the getaway trips with her friends. So she chose the course of action that would give her optimum peace, because that was what she most desired.

If my client got out of the house on the weekends, her husband would get some well-deserved time to himself. He also sacrificed a lot for the family, as he explained when he joined his wife in a later session. He worked a lot and needed a lot of alone time as well, to recharge his batteries. He wasn't really a people person, and his wife always wanted to do all sorts of fun stuff. He usually came along, because the only thing he hated more than doing things he didn't feel like doing was having arguments. As I said, we always weigh up the pros and cons. We do it unconsciously, with every action we undertake. We always make a psychological investment. Anyway, I didn't think I needed to teach these people to start putting themselves first; the complaint, as always, was not the problem.

> We always unconsciously choose the behaviour that brings us the most psychological satisfaction, the behaviour that serves our motivation best.

## The motivations exposed

Both partners in this relationship complained that they sacrificed too much of themselves for others. The problem however, seemed to have to do with how they, in their own ways, were trying to avoid confrontations. That was how they both attempted to keep doing what they wanted, each of them driven by a completely different motivation. The wife didn't like complications, and wanted to keep the peace at all costs (ideal image). That meant she needed to avoid conflict and friction, but she still wanted to be able to go out and have fun as well. So she chose to take her space indirectly. She tried to have her cake and eat it too, and that was starting to take its toll. The husband really just wanted to have the space do his own things. That was why he preferred being alone, because then he wouldn't have to deal with people who wouldn't understand him anyway. He just wanted to be able to be himself (ideal image).

Whatever their motivations, both of them benefited from avoiding having a conversation about these things, afraid it would turn into a conflict. The wife was afraid of discord; the husband was afraid of rejection, it turned out later. These kinds of things don't help a marriage. Partners can even start hating each other over situations like this! That's because both sides keep secretly hoping the other person will fix the problem they have unconsciously created, thereby allowing relatively minor problems to grow to epic proportions. The wife wanted harmony 24/7; she wanted to avoid all possible conflict. She appeared quiet, but inside the dissatisfaction and unease only mounted. The husband wanted to be able to truly be himself 24/7. It was difficult for him to be truly engaged with his wife, and he would more and more often reject the fun plans she came up with. In his opinion most people were pretty fake, so why should he invest in them? He increasingly kept his distance in the hope she would leave him be. If she did go her own way, then that wouldn't feel right either. His somewhat perfunctory care of the children was a kind of unconscious blackmail; it created the friction that she was so sensitive to, and so the vicious cycle was kept alive. Now, you'd be forgiven for thinking these people are very unpleasant, or selfish, but in truth they are just doing what everybody does; trying to live their lives with the best of intentions.

We often chase after an unattainable ideal, and this causes frustration. Altering your ideals instantly lightens your load, and solves many complaints at once, forever!

## Hidden contracts

Just like other couples, this pair made many hidden contracts over the course of their relationship. "If you don't nag me about this, then I won't cause a fuss over that." "If you come along to a party every now and again, then I'll be home on time to do the lunchboxes for the kids." "If I work a lot, then I'll need time to myself. So if you want to have fun with your friends, then make sure I'm not bothered by it."

Interesting. And as long as it works, this is fine. For this couple, over time their bargains caused increasing dissatisfaction. This makes sense; after all, their whole system was based on their avoiding each other, which usually doesn't help a relationship. On top of this, the patterns in your relationship almost always repeat themselves in your career, family, and all other aspects of your life. Eventually this will take its toll, because it costs ever more energy to keep avoiding something that is simply a part of life, in this case rejection and stress.

## The real problem exposed

To recap, both people were champions of conflict avoidance, but for different reasons. The motor of your behaviour always lies in your unconscious motivation. The wife turned out to have a type 9 drive and the husband a type 4. The first step was for both to receive an insight into their unconscious system. They recognised their basic patterns and they could see the real problem behind their complaints. That's what we started working with. The wife learnt that her motivation caused her to always strive for harmony and peace, and that this was the reason she would rather subdue her opinions than express them. She did have an opinion however, so on the inside her anger only grew, while on the outside she appeared relaxed and pleasant. Step by step, we taught her to vocalise her disturbances and dissatisfaction. The husband learnt to engage more with her, to stay connected. His motivation meant he had an interest in keeping others from getting too close. After all, when you connect with someone, they might reject you; that was a risk he wasn't willing to take. For that reason he would always behave merely appropriately towards others, rather than making an effort to relate to them. Unfortunately, on the inside, this caused him to grow increasingly unfeeling, which, of course, didn't exactly benefit his relationship with his wife.

Through learning each other's unconscious drives, this couple became much more understanding. They also found out how much they had in common; both of them, inspired by entirely different convictions, feared confrontation and intensity of emotion. During our coaching we focused on identifying those convictions, as well as adjusting them (I'll delve into this more under principles 3 and 4). You become less critical towards others when you understand them; this created an opening and made communication possible again. And yes, that does a relationship good!

This isn't some fairytale; it's a true story about the effect of receiving an insight into your motivations. When you find the real problem – and the real problem always springs from your unconscious motivation – then you resolve many different complaints in one go. The husband, for example, chose to apply his newfound knowledge at work as well, and by being more engaged there he even received a promotion. He started to appreciate human contact and didn't feel rejected as easily. Contact with his wife in particular became more rewarding for him, now that she expressed herself more. Finally she became more conspicuous in his eyes, became more human, more real. He loved that. The wife improved as well; becoming more visible and present benefited her tremendously.

In the weekends, the kids often stayed with their grandmother. That way the parents, who used to "sacrifice" so much, could have some much-needed time to themselves. These days they increasingly use that time to come closer together as well. Grandma was fine with everything; the more the merrier, she always said. She relished it, which is why I never saw her in my practice, even though she was probably the one who sacrificed the most. She didn't mind that, though. She loved taking care of others; it was part of her motivation. Anticipating the expectations of people around her is what kept her going. Being loyal and putting others before herself were totally her thing. She enjoyed having company and hated being alone. As long as she was busy she was happy, then she wouldn't have to feel her own insecurity. Grandmother later turned out to be a type 6. It only goes to show, the complaint is never the problem!

## Conclusion

A good coach always looks for the problem behind the complaint; the complaint has grown from the unconscious convictions and ideals of the client. If you know someone's unconscious motivation, you know their convictions and you can tell what ideals he or she is striving for. You will be able to see how that person creates their own problems, and the complaints that spring from them. You can truly help people that way, especially because you're not working to resolve the complaint, but the real problem. This fixes many different complaints at once because you are breaking a pattern, structurally!

## PRINCIPLE 3

### BEHIND EVERY PROBLEM THERE IS AN UNCONCSIOUS CONVICTION

The previous example showed that the complaint is not the problem, and that behind every problem there is an unconscious conviction. One of the wife's limiting convictions was, "If I express myself, then that will lead to conflict." The husband limited himself with the conviction, "If I am truly myself, then I will be rejected." They came to see a coach because they were sacrificing so much for others; that was the complaint. A coach could walk into that trap wide-eyed. Or even worse, you could start feeling sorry for one of the couple, perhaps because you recognise something of yourself in them. There is always a temptation to project one of your own standards or judgements onto the situation, or to start paying attention to the content. Be aware of this, because before you know it, you end up working on the complaint instead of the problem. If a coach had focused on the content in this situation, he would have attempted to teach his clients to stand up for themselves more. He would have taught them to stop putting themselves last. Unfortunately, this wouldn't have helped them one bit. They simply couldn't have done anything with the new information if they didn't first understand which limiting conviction was blocking them from change. Only when they recognise that can they start seeing the real problem for what it is, and start taking responsibility for their part in it.

### You see: I'm right!

Convictions are generalisations about reality. We pretend things are always a certain way, as if the generalisation always holds true, and we make sure we prove ourselves correct. This means we are always right! Convictions often take the form of an if/then statement, one

> Convictions are generalisations about ourselves, others and the world that we make sure are proven true. We do not see the rest.

that we present as truth. However, they are often easy to disprove. For example, a conviction might be, "If I don't do it, then nothing will happen." The chances are very good that if you have this conviction, it has been proven to you time and time again. The funny thing is that when something goes against this conviction, you barely even notice it. It simply will not register, because it doesn't fit your worldview. Only the things that fit our worldview usually make it past our filter.

It is essential to realise that you are, be it unconsciously, driven by convictions that you always prove correct. If you believe that you always need to be strong because in the end we are all on our own in life, then that will hold true. If you are convinced that nobody will really understand you anyway, then you are unconsciously investing in rejection. "You see," you'll end up saying, "I am different, nobody understands me." You don't even notice the times that you are understood by others, because they don't make it past your filter. You only register the things that confirm your self-image and your vision of the world. This is called selective perception. The lens through which you see the world is quite different from mine. One thing we have in common, however, is that the things we think about ourselves, others and life in general, we make come true. In many ways, our convictions are self-fulfilling prophecies. Everyone makes their own convictions come true, so everyone is always right.

Our view on things gives us guidance and structure, which is why we all want to believe our vision is the right one. This means, however, that it is difficult to realise when to lower the bar, when to cut your losses and adjust your expectations. It's difficult for us to accept the situation as it is, even when it differs from your ideal image. Like everyone, you are chasing a dream that has little to do with reality.

## Surviving instead of living

Limiting convictions keep you from experiencing the here and now; they keep you in survival mode. You keep striving for more, better and different things, forgetting to live life to the fullest. Your limiting convictions make it very difficult for you to accept life as it is, which in turn causes you frustration, pain, sadness and fear. Your unconscious convictions keep you in survival mode, when you could be out living your life.

To illustrate this I will take the example of a friend of mine who tried to explain to me that her overly caring, solicitous behaviour was due to her having had a very dominant father. If you have read this far into the book, you will probably understand that I didn't exactly see the logic in that. As I explained under principle 1, it isn't your circumstances that determine who you are, it's how you deal with them. Furthermore, I had my own version of a dominant father at home and it only served to make me rebellious and defiant. There was one thing I knew for certain: the complaint wasn't the problem.

Back to my friend: her psychotherapist had taught her that her tendency to protect her mother during childhood had led her to display the same behaviour towards her friends now. This is how she ended up with lots of rather unequal friendships that cost her a lot of energy. Now she was confused; her NLP coach had explained to her that the root of her problems existed in the way she thought. Anyway, she couldn't care less; she had had a lovely "rebirthing" session the previous week and now she was totally in touch with herself again. She just had to take more space and signal her boundaries better, and she was completely ready for it.

> When you know your unconscious motivation, you know which ideal images you chase after 24/7, and which convictions keep them in place.

Her boss at work could say what he wanted, she was not going let herself go crazy doing extra overtime anymore. Those silly friends that kept asking for her help at every turn could finally learn to figure it out for themselves. She was only going to have equal friendships from now on, with people that also paid attention to her for a change. Then she would finally have more time and space for herself!

I was impressed, especially because she started by cutting off a few friendships that had been on the back burner for a while. The way she chose to do it was a bit half-hearted in my opinion: "Sorry, I don't have time right now," "I have to finish a few other things first," "...busy at work", "I need some time to myself..." It was all fairly careful and even a bit defensive. However, it was only a first step and she was convinced her friends had understood the message. More importantly, it did appear that there was now a bit more free space in her schedule. The problem was that she was now bothered by a terrible sense of guilt, which she found difficult to deal with.

We spoke about this for evenings on end, how much it plagued her how rude she'd been to a few friends. What's more, her transformation ended up costing me quite a bit of time as well, because I, for different reasons, have my own issues concerning setting my boundaries. At this rate I was developing a problem of my own.

Guilty feelings aside, my friend didn't really know what to do with her newfound free space and time. In no time at all, she had arranged all kinds of new obligations for herself. Now that her friends weren't so dependent on her anymore, she had more time for her family. She had recently been feeling very guilty and neglectful of them, so it was great she could now be more involved. Before she knew it, she was caught up in the middle of her cousin's divorce, and to make matters worse her sister asked her to be a maid of honour at her wedding. My friend was flattered; her sister is quite critical and chose to trust her with this important task. She was even a bit proud of being asked and said yes before she could think twice.

There she was, on the couch, with a stack of wedding magazines on her lap; on top was a book titled *Divorce without damage*. Even more tired than before, she explained to her coach how she stopped letting people walk all over her, and that she had become much more assertive towards her employer. She also told him how she had cut off a few burdensome friendships. The complaints she came in with were solved! Only, the problem was still there...

## Turbulence!

Even though it can be useful to learn to set boundaries, most of us do not foresee the consequences it might have. Signalling boundaries often means cutting things and people off; it means staking out your territory, creating less space for the other and more for yourself. That's scary for many people, for a diverse range of reasons. One person could be afraid of the reactions of others; someone might reject you or become angry when you set your boundaries. Someone else might not have a clue about what to do with the extra time and possibilities. There are all kinds of possible reasons why someone might have trouble taking their space, establishing boundaries, but whatever that reason is, it comes from our unconscious motivations and convictions!

When my friend learnt to set boundaries, her autopilot made sure that the space that was created was immediately filled up again. The new space may have had the appearance of newfound freedom at first, but her autopilot thought, "Turbulence! That's not how I programmed you; get back to doing what you're good at. Stop that nonsense and just be there for others, you've done it all your life!"

On a conscious level my friend truly wanted more freedom. The thing she overlooked at first though, was that more freedom and space also meant more time to herself. She wasn't very good at that. When she was alone she started feeling her own unrest, her own needs and desires, and she couldn't deal with those very well. That's why she made sure she always had people and projects going on that could comfortably distract her from her own troubles.

## You are what you think

One of my friend's complaints was "I let others rule my life too much." The real problem behind this complaint was "If I can't add anything to the lives of others, I feel lost." Her coach would have done better to deal with that problem.

Through finding out my friend's convictions I found out she is a type 2 person, and that she unconsciously wants to be needed by others. That's how she hopes to deserve people's love and respect. She is always very thoughtful, pays close attention to the needs of others, and in doing so attracts many people who come to lean on her heavily. She, in turn, is disappointed because she doesn't get enough from those relationships herself. Time and time again she has ended up at a point where she felt exhausted and empty. It isn't easy for her to ask for help herself, so you would think it a small miracle that she even kept going into therapy anyway. Actually, there is an unconscious reason even for that. Asking for help is only possible when you pay for it; that's how she keeps herself out of the other person's debt. It's another conviction of type 2 people: when somebody helps you, you must do something back for them a.s.a.p. It just goes to show how our unconscious convictions determine every little aspect of our lives.

In order to get to the real problem it's important to understand how someone thinks. This means finding out the convictions that keep the problem in place.

Many therapists and coaches later, my friend still ended up empty-handed. This only served to confirm the conviction that she couldn't lean on anyone else. I know her father too, kind of a nice guy. He can be a bit cynical every now and then but he usually makes people laugh. It didn't amuse her mother, however, and my friend was always very concerned about this. She still automatically jumps to defend her mother when her father is having one laugh too many at the expense of others. This is what she calls dominant. That's how easily we use those kinds of words. They are catchall phrases that can easily sidetrack you from the issue at hand.

Part of a coach's job is to always expose catchall phrases; these are hollow words that have a different definition for everyone. When you continue to probe and examine these words you naturally end up with the underlying convictions.

A good coach would have asked my friend, "What do you mean by dominant?" My friend meant, "He doesn't take into account my mother's feelings enough." A nice follow-up question would have been, "Why does that affect you?" Then my friend would have probably answered, "Because I think you need to be considerate of others in life, otherwise you are selfish." This is how you automatically end up at the convictions that lead to the real problem. If you are considerate of others you deserve their love; that's one of type 2's core convictions. Another one is, when others are disadvantaged, it's up to you to relieve their wanting. This is why my friend jumped into situations where her mother was being short-changed in her eyes. Additionally, she was the one that could make a difference in her cousin's divorce, she knew a good mediator somewhere that could help. It's only logical that her sister wanted her to arrange the wedding; my friend always takes everyone's wishes into account. Her sister was quite right to pick her and it only fed my friend's pride; she was the only one asked, after all. Everything would turn out fine in the end; she was onto it!

"It will be fine!" was one of her favourite expressions, which is why nobody ever really worried about her. Everything always turned out fine. If you knew her motivations, you would see how she continually overexerted herself by exaggerating her qualities. That's also where the real problem behind her complaint lies. Behind the complaint, "I have too many unequal and strenuous relationships," is the problem, "I always need to make a difference in the lives of others." Behind that is the conviction, "Only when I contribute positively to the lives of others will I deserve their love." Behind the complaint, "I am bothered by my father's dominance," is the problem, "I think he doesn't take into account my mother's feelings enough," and the conviction, "Whenever you say something, you must always take into account the other person's feelings." This is another one of type 2's core convictions and it explains much of her behaviour. Adjusting this conviction would give her a lot of space to breathe. She would solve many of her complaints at once. More about this is explained under principle 4.

## Team building

Most businesses spend lots of money on corporate events, outings and team building activities. They rent out a hotel in a nice location for two days, take the whole department down there, and a month later nobody remembers what the outing was about. The conversations at the hotel bar that first night, though, they remember those. Who would have thought that that particular colleague would come to life so much after a few beers? And it is impressive how human the manager can turn out to be when he relaxes a bit. It's a shame that the next morning he is back to his usual unapproachable self, just like everyone else. It's especially disappointing when you remember that the goal of these events is usually to communicate more effectively as a team, in accordance with the Rotenberg hexagon. Ever heard of it?

Some time ago I gave a workshop for the management team for a large telecommunications company from the Netherlands. The director was really into Twitter at that time, which was clear from the moment he walked in the door. Somewhat reluctantly he put his iPhone away in order to shake my hand. As soon as we had started handing out training material he was back to his phone, busily communicating with the outside world. Around him colleagues stood talking in groups.

In a formal opening speech he explained the importance of good communication, how he looked forward to getting to know himself and his co-workers better. "Everything begins with self-knowledge," he exclaimed enthusiastically; he had read that on Twitter. A friend, a famous management guru, said it. He found it an appropriate slogan for this event.

During training I regularly saw him look at his phone. He had put it on silent, but the messages kept coming in. He was first out of his seat during every break to read and answer his email. His colleagues, still pondering the new self-insight they had received, gave him as wide a berth as possible. They didn't want to disturb him. Now and then he excitedly shared the latest message he had sent into the world, and the responses that had followed. The colleagues smiled appropriately at the boss and his toy, a man in constant contact with the world, but unreachable for those around him.

## "Twitter Theo" comes back to humanity

After the break I thought it was time to ask him about his behaviour. I explained that I was confused: he said he wanted better communication, and I thought that was a beautiful goal to have, but he seemed more involved with his phone than his colleagues; how did he see that? What did the others think of it?

"Whatever floats his boat," said one colleague, afraid that his words would come back to bite him later. "That's the way he's always been," said another one, trying to play it safe as well. I decided on a different approach: "Take a new sheet of paper and write down anonymously how you feel about your director's tweeting."

That approach was more productive. The general feeling was that everyone was fed up with his behaviour. Most also thought that it hurt his credibility that he kept talking about communication when he was unreachable himself. The man seemed shocked. He had had no idea that this was the effect of his behaviour; he honestly meant that. People often do not realise that their behaviour has consequences, that you can't say one thing and do another. People will always judge each other on incongruent behaviour.

Next, I asked the question, "What would you want from your boss?" Answers included more contact, easier access to his time when questions needed answering, more communication in general and more interest in what they where up to on a daily basis. The boss listened intently; he was all ears and hadn't looked at his metal friend in over half an hour. He tried to process everything his colleagues said. "Is that really how it looks when I do that?" he asked surprised. "Yes," a colleague said, "and it's not just us who notice this. They don't call you Twitter Theo for nothing." The man blushed sheepishly.

It was the right moment to share something about this man's motivations, the explanation for all his behaviour! This is how he discovered that he is actually quite scared of being wholly present. He knew these kinds of meetings were important, he had read that in one of his books about management, but he had been somewhat dreading it from the start. He learnt that part of him spent all day monitoring the reactions of others to make sure things didn't get too personal. He saw that he had been doing this unconsciously all this time. His motivation meant that he needed to stay independent of the emotional world at all times; it meant that he preferred to focus on the objective world instead. He preferred to be somewhat invisible, to be a spectator rather than a participant.

For the first time his colleagues saw a human being in him, someone who struggled with himself, who was afraid to become conspicuous and hid behind his mobile phone. When we further explained his unconscious motivations it became crystal clear to everyone what the root of Theo's behaviour was. When you understand someone, you become less critical towards him or her. The atmosphere changed immediately. Now there was true communication.

The communication became even better when the others started to find their own unconscious motivation systems. One of them, for example, found out that, based on his motivation, he felt the need for a great deal of recognition and appreciation. He also sought to establish and maintain connection with others at all times; that was what made him feel safe and secure. So that was the reason why he, particularly, was so annoyed by his boss's behaviour. However hard he tried to establish contact with his employer, it wouldn't work. It made him very insecure. Now it was easier for him to say where his own behaviour came from. Yes, beautiful things happen when people discover their unconscious motivations. Suddenly they understand much better which elements of the communication have to do with their own struggles, and which belong to the other person.

## Fear of contact

We gave the director in question more insight into his unconscious motivations and convictions in a number of sessions. He started to see how, as a type 5 person, he would rather focus on the world around him than on the interior world. He used to think emotions couldn't get him anywhere. Unconsciously he always strived to be reasonable and rational. He realised all too well that keeping this up was costing him ever more energy. He sincerely longed for contact, but he was also afraid of it. The limiting conviction keeping this fear alive was, if you let people in, then things quickly become intense and emotional. During our sessions we worked on adjusting this conviction. After all, when you let people in, it may also give you pleasant connections with others, or emotional and mental nourishment. Twitter had become an escape for him: still in contact with others, but not too close. He saw that now.

A year later we were invited for another company outing with the same director. This time he greeted us warmly when we walked in. He opened the session by sharing with his colleagues the insights he had acquired. He talked about the limiting convictions he had discovered in himself and how he was working on breaking through those patterns. He also suggested that their phones be turned off for the duration of the training; they would only distract from the communication!

## Conclusion

Behind every problem is a limiting conviction; that's a comforting thought, don't you think? Perhaps you don't have to give up on your marriage, move house, change jobs; perhaps all you need to do is find out how you work. Then you will see your problems in a new light.

Helpful questions to ask yourself are: What am I doing to keep this problem alive? Which limiting conviction lies behind my problem? Which ideal image am I fighting to uphold? What is coming from me and what is caused by those around me? This is an honest way of seeing that is conducive to happiness, because you start experiencing the influence you have over your own life. You are the one that holds the key to adjusting your limiting convictions. That's what the next chapter is about.

## PRINCIPLE 4

### THE ADJUSTMENT OF A CONVICTION LEADS TO LASTING CHANGE

It is a coach's job to find out the client's unconscious motivations, to discover the cause of the stomach ache, if you will. In order to do this, the coach must study which limiting convictions keep the problem in place and expose the story behind a complaint. That story comes from our motivations and ideals, which are really convictions about the world around us. A conviction that causes more pain than pleasure can be called "limiting." A limiting conviction holds a problem in place, prevents it from being solved. Conversely, you solve a problem by adjusting the limiting conviction. However, your client needs to be motivated enough to want to do this. In practice this usually means his problem needs to bother him enough.

Limiting convictions are the ones that cost us more than they bring us. This type of conviction keeps a problem alive and causes frustration; the motor that gets us moving!

In the most recent example, under principle 4, you could read how a type 5 manager carefully adjusted a conviction, and what good this brought him. The moment people see exactly what they have been doing all this time, and realise the strategy isn't productive anymore, most of them are motivated enough to look at their own behaviour with a critical eye.

When people refuse to face the facts, nature often helps them on their way a bit: they feel tired, get vague health complaints, or simply do not feel happy in their skins. They become irritable and get annoyed over the tiniest things. We human beings are very good at denial, repression, distraction and many other forms of behaviour that help us so we do not have to acknowledge that something about our behaviour is no longer working for us. Behaviour that stops us from accepting that our current way of being is unsustainable.

Sometimes people are sent to meet with a coach by their partners or employers. Often those clients even think those that sent them are exaggerating: "There's always something, why make a big deal out of it?" That's how accustomed we are to living half a life. We accept it because we do not know any better, we don't know life can be happier, more rewarding, more fulfilling.

> **It isn't our unconscious motivations that block us from having better lives; it's a lack of self-insight. Insight leads to perspective!**

When you see the extent to which your motivations rule you, you'll see how you, together with everyone else, run the risk of becoming a caricature of yourself. We all run the risk of repeating ourselves and getting stuck following the same pattern all our lives, just because we don't know any better. When you start to see those patterns, motivation to change them for the better automatically follows!

## Happy-go-lucky

Take, for example, the manager that came to us exhausted from being unable to run his team. He described himself as a cheerful leader who gave everyone the space and freedom they needed. He genuinely believed that people performed better when they were given free rein in their work. Rules were more like guidelines; you shouldn't abide by them too much, was one of his convictions. This again shows how our convictions drive us to do what we do. If you give people freedom they perform better, so every Friday this manager organised an office get-together. This event was always good fun and would often run late. The office atmosphere was truly great, that wasn't the problem. People had started cutting corners, though; profits went down and deadlines were often not met. The man had taken several management courses already, which would usually focus on helping him bring more structure into the company. For a while this would work, and yes, things would run a bit more efficiently then, but invariably the office was back to its old ways in a matter of months. This makes sense; the manager wasn't really a structured person. If you believed, like he did, that rules are really more like guidelines, then applying structure to a company would be outside your realm of capabilities as well. After all, applying structure has to do with enforcing a set of rules. As I explained before, our unconscious convictions are always stronger than our conscious will. To rephrase that, somebody might give you tips and advice, but your autopilot makes sure you are back to doing what you're used to in no time.

## Outsourcing your self-development

Our manager had hired an office manager, someone who was good at applying structure. That seemed easiest to him. Yes that's how we humans like to do things: we outsource a little piece of our own development. In fact, most marriages are based on exactly this principle.

The office manager liked rules; he was a type 1 person, to be precise. One of his unconscious convictions was, "If you are clear with people, they know what's in store for them and are easier to manage." Structure was his middle name. For a while it seemed a miracle solution, the right kind of person in the right place, but now they were having trouble.

From the very first, the office manager had been thoroughly vexed by his supervisor's behaviour. There were many things in the office he thought could be improved upon, and he had applied a clear structure, with straightforward agreements. This was all in vain; his boss would not be told what to do. At first he had tried not to get too annoyed with his supervisor. Self-control is a priority for type 1 people. You don't show your emotions at the drop of a hat; you keep them under control and only express them when they are appropriate. Type 1 knows without question whether or not it's appropriate; he has very clear standards for that purpose. Every response is first measures by their "standards bureau".

In order to somewhat restrain his boss's happy-go-lucky behaviour, the office manager clamped down on the rules a bit harder. This is turn caused more resistance. Not a single agreement was kept. Mistakes were made, something that enraged the office manager even further, and he worked late nearly every evening to repair the damage his supervisor had caused during the day. He just felt responsible for the business. He kept his anger inside for a long time but last week, when he had to keep a client waiting for an hour, that was the final straw. He had ended up reprimanding his boss in front of the client, and now he was embarrassed about that; he shouldn't have let himself go like that. Thankfully his supervisor took it lightly.

## Over- and under-functioning

"That man is so rigid," the manager complained to us in his first conversation. Admittedly, profits were up and employees were taking their work more seriously and keeping agreements better. But all the hard work meant most people were leaving the office on time on Friday, so there wasn't much left of the office get-together. The atmosphere was tense and it bothered him. More importantly, he felt rushed. He had thought work would become less demanding for him with the new employee but the opposite was true. More demands were put on him every day.

The moment people come into contact with each other, a pattern of over- and under-functioning is created. Systems have the tendency to strive for balance. Imbalance is immediately compensated for. The manager's breezy attitude made his office manager become serious enough for the both of them. The more chaotic the manager became, the more structure his right-hand man would apply. That's how systems work.

This manager had done a whole bunch of courses and training. He also married a principled and straightforward wife (who would keep an eye on structure so he could keep playing). Over time she also became less patient with his non-committal behaviour, even though that was what had once attracted her to him. She was fairly strict and a happy and relaxed husband seemed like the perfect deal to her. As I have said, we like to outsource a bit of our development. Unfortunately, in the long run this hardly ever works; we only keep getting more stuck in our patterns. This is how the wife became ever more critical and sharp, even though she was first attracted to her husband because he made her feel more relaxed. He never took things too seriously, and at first she loved that about him; now she sometimes even hated him for it.

## Pain avoidance as a life strategy

When you gain insight into your motivations, you won't just discover what you are unconsciously aiming for; you will also find out what it is you are trying to avoid. When you come to understand this system, you will see how that avoidance is usually what gets you in the end. That's because nearly all your energy is devoted to it. Negative energy, to be precise, because the things we try to avoid in life are actually just a part of it; it's a war we can never win. This is how we quickly realised we were dealing with a type 7 person. The manager is someone who, more than anything, wants to avoid being restricted. He would give everything (and in fact was well on his way to doing so) to be free and experience as much pleasure as possible. A life without pain, wouldn't we all love that?

His non-committal attitude ended up costing him his job, and nearly his marriage as well. The complaint was the same: both his employer and his wife thought he lacked dedication. For a type 7 person, commitment means restriction, limitation. When you commit to something, you restrict yourself, is one of type 7's limiting convictions. This conviction is limiting because you end up causing more pain than pleasure when you never commit to anything or anyone. Thankfully, this was something he was starting to see for himself.

Because the man wanted more freedom in life, he started his own business. A clothing shop, "time for something entirely different," he thought. You should see this one coming miles away: he is, unfortunately, stuck in exactly the same predicament. Having your own business is no walk in the park, as he soon found out. It requires hard work and devotion and there were many elements he did not see coming. His lack of commitment ended up short-changing him in this project as well as the last.

> You can change whatever you like about your environment; you bring yourself and your unconscious convictions along. Unconsciously you keep working towards the same conclusion.

You can change jobs, partners, or change something else about yourself in life; your problems are usually there to stay. The new clothing shop briefly seemed a success . He was creative, combining some exclusive brands with affordable options. Actually, the shop was a bit of everything, because that fitted him best. He called himself a generalist. I hear that most often from people who do not like to focus, and so don't like to commit themselves. Accounting fell by the wayside now and then in the clothing shop; it wasn't really his thing. He was also a bit scared of confronting people who had unpaid accounts, he preferred to keep things fun. His tendency towards excess caused him to continually overstock.

## Letting in what you have been avoiding

We taught this man about his unconscious motivations. Through us he realised how his limitless desire for pleasure and freedom had caused him to avoid anything that restricted him. He also realised how that was exactly how he had ended up limiting himself tremendously. He had made a mess of things, leaving him out of work, with an angry wife; he was totally stuck. He started to see how he had spent his entire life avoiding pain. This is another catchall phrase by the way; in the world of type 7 it means anything that doesn't bring immediate pleasure. Life must be fun, light, cheerful and pleasurable, not serious, rigid, restrictive, boring, dreary, painful or heavy. And yes, there is a price to pay for that.

Step by step this man learnt to take himself more seriously, and at first that hurt. But the pain didn't last long because relief soon followed. It didn't kill him and what was more, it actually made him feel better to take his own pain seriously. After all, he hurt just like everyone else, things would bother him, and he would get disappointed or sad. Over time it cost him more and more energy to keep pushing that all away.

> It is only worthwhile changing a limiting conviction if you are prepared to let something in that you have been trying to avoid. That's when you break through a pattern and when you find balance.

To his amazement, people started taking his needs into account. This way he effortlessly adjusted a conviction. When you take yourself seriously, life gets heavy, was one of his core convictions. The new one went, "When you take yourself seriously, people start taking your needs into account." That's another thing he had managed for himself; everyone saw him as the jolly clown of the bunch. He was slowly getting sick of that image. And guess what? Now that he had become more serious, his wife had started becoming more cheerful. Just the other day she said, "Don't take life so seriously honey; there is always a silver lining!" "She got that on from me," he laughed, "and now she's giving it back!" This is a typical example of over- and under-functioning!

The man was surprised that it was so effective to adjust your motivations. He now realised that every upside had a downside and has become much more realistic. That's exactly why everything has become a lot easier for him. Everything is allowed now: sadness as well as happiness, pain as well as pleasure. They are a part of life and there is no escaping it.

Last week we had our final session and he said, "I always used to think that if I didn't take life too seriously I would be happy. Now I know and feel that if I take myself and life seriously, then I feel alive, and that makes me happy. You should try it sometime," he smiled at me. "It's a real pick-me-up."

## Conclusion

This example shows perfectly how we end up faced with the things we try to avoid. The manager was stuck in the middle of his pain, even though he was trying his hardest to stay away from it. His excessive need for pleasure made him unconsciously cause more and more pain and heaviness. It's our common fate: we all unconsciously work towards our avoidances. When you start seeing this happen, the motivation to do something about it follows. It's essential to understand what it is you want to avoid. Seeing how we unconsciously avoid things can save lives! The moment you understand what you do, and what you are avoiding, you give yourself the chance to adjust a conviction. Usually that means letting something into your life you have been trying to avoid. It takes some getting used to, but you will end up the better version of yourself.

The great Dutch football coach and part-time philosopher Johan Cruyff said it well: "You only see it when you get it." That's just the way it is! Even more importantly, from that moment on you will be unable to un-see it. That's how it works when you adjust limiting convictions. That's why the change is irreversible and why it gives lasting results.

## PRINCIPLE 5

### THERE ARE NINE UNCONSCIOUS MOTIVATIONS

The idea that there are only nine motivations and nine personality types might take some getting used to, but that's the way it is. One of those motivations fits you and how you see the world. That doesn't mean we all behave similarly, however! That would be too simply put. My sister and I are both women, for example, but we are entirely different people. That's how you need to look at motivations. You and I might have the same motivations but our behaviour could be entirely different. The opposite is also true: two people with different motivations can behave almost exactly the same. As we have said before, behaviour is interchangeable. This makes it completely useless to analyse a person based on behaviour alone, even though, unfortunately, this often happens when you go to see a coach. If you really want to do someone justice, you must learn to see through his or her behaviour. This sounds more complicated than it is. It means you shouldn't get distracted by the content but should look for the way someone interprets things. Listening for the way somebody literally gives meaning to the world around him or her will lead you to his or her unconscious convictions about that world. Their convictions will lead you to their unconscious motivation.

> Typing people on their behaviour alone is useless; behaviour is interchangeable, it says little about your motivations.

Now, if you think this sounds easier said than done, you'd be right. It takes education and experience to be able to do this properly. Please allow someone with training in this subject to guide you if you are interested in learning more about unconscious motivations. The best way to learn to accurately analyse and guide others is from an expert with experience in motivation-conscious coaching and personality typing. It's more than worth it!

Let's also be clear on the fact that it is very difficult to accurately identify your own unconscious motivation. We all have a blind spot that prevents us from seeing what we are doing while we are doing it.

Instead, we usually recognise something of our own behaviour in every personality type description. Still, it can be fun and rewarding to take on the challenge of tying to find your own motivation. This means training yourself to read behind the words to find the underlying motivation.

Unfortunately there is no other way to explain the motivations than in words, and so we end up describing behaviour. We do, however, always explain the motivation behind the behaviour. When you take on the challenge, remember that your motivation is at work 24/7. Keep asking yourself, "Do I always do this? Is this a pattern in my life? Is this where my issues and problems come from?"

Don't forget to enjoy the search! In any case you will learn that there are nine ways of dealing with life, nine filters. You will also learn that your filter determines how you interpret the world. It's good fun, getting to know the nine unconscious motivation systems. Take your time discovering your own, or enlist the help of an expert!

## The unconscious motivation: our unconscious coach!

Our unconscious motivation is in fact an unconscious coach that helps us follow our survival strategy 24/7. It keeps us on track and within our comfort zone, so we keep doing what we do best. When you understand which unconscious coach is guiding you, you can take back control and make conscious decisions. I explain more about this in the last chapter.

This book also goes into the added value of motivation-conscious coaching. When speaking about this form of coaching, I sometimes mention another kind of unconscious coach: the professional coach who is unaware of his own motivations, and attempts to help others without knowing himself. We believe there are negative consequences to this type of coaching, which I have listed in the chapter "Coach alert: Beware the unconscious coach!".

First, though, we will meet the unconscious coaches inside ourselves, our unconscious motivation. The description of the personality types explains how this unconscious coach attempts to keep us well within our comfort zones. Welcome to the world of the nine personality types!

> There are nine motivations, nine survival strategies, nine worldviews, nine sets of convictions, nine personality types, nine ideal images, nine filters, nine unconscious coaches!

# 3
# Meet the nine unconscious coaches

## Earning your right to exist

It's no easy feat to discover your own unconscious motivation; it's unconscious for a reason. And yet we must start somewhere. That's why I have globally outlined each personality type's self-image, as well as their most important convictions. This illustrates each type's ideal worldview, and that which they care to avoid in life.

An ideal image is a clear image of yourself and the world; one that you wish to realise 24/7. By definition, this is unattainable. That's what frustrates us in life, and what makes us work hard to try and make things how we think they should be. We focus on changing the world to fit our ideal image, instead of questioning the image itself. This is a vicious cycle. It is understandable that we do things this way; our ideal image gives us structure and security. We derive our self-image from it, and more importantly, our right to exist. Our unconscious motivation describes our favourite survival strategy. It's how we imagine earning the right to be. If I do things a certain way, then I deserve to exist. That's the unconscious conviction at the base of every personality type. What exactly is that way of doing things? That depends on your unconscious motivation. One person might think it means being loyal to others, and not counting on himself too much; another thinks he needs to trust only himself and nobody else. Yet another personality type strives to do everything absolutely perfectly, not to make a single mistake. There are nine different survival strategies like these, nine unconscious coaches: nine personality types.

## WELCOME TO THE WORLD OF TYPE 1

### EVERYTHING CAN BE IMPROVED!

***If I do the right thing and meet my own strict standards 24/7, then I will be perfect. I won't have to face my own imperfection and I will be able to survive safely.***

Imagine always being in touch with your own imperfection. Also imagine continually noting the shortcomings of the world around you, those points where reality consistently differs from your ideals, your personal standard. This frustrates and irritates. In fact, it angers you. Irritation is type 1's middle name, and with good reason. Irritation is nothing if not pent up anger, the motor that drives type 1 to improve himself and his surroundings 24/7. He does this to make those surroundings better meet his standards. Everything can be improved! Actually, everything *must* be improved. This also happens to be type 1's greatest strength: an enormous drive to push himself and others to a higher level, not to accept a world filled with imperfection. The standard is perfection, and type 1 always strives to meet that standard.

***If reality deviates from your standards, then that's irritating and something must be done about it.***

Perfection is another word for 'doing the right thing'. In the world of type 1 this means meeting your own standards. Every time he manages to meet his standards, the type 1 person experiences a little bit of perfection, a little bit of what he loves most. What exactly is the 'right' thing to do? What is the standard? Type 1 just knows. A standard is nothing more than an opinion about what things should be like; and for the type 1 person, this opinion is always present. He simply cannot perceive anyone or anything without some form of judgement. Let us not forget that judgement, or if you will, a standard, gives us guidance and structure. This side of the line is good, the other, wrong. Perfect if you like your world clear-cut. Herein lies a taste of type 1's tendency to binary, black-and-white thinking; things are either right or wrong, black or white. In every instance, this type will question whether his standard has been met, and what could, and should, be improved upon.

***If you meet your own standards, then you are doing the right thing.***

Type 1 people are idealists rather than realists; this critical personality type sets the bar high, often too high. This is the reason their standards often aren't met, and why complete satisfaction is a rare occurrence for type 1. They will usually see a mistake somewhere, an imperfection, and have little trouble connecting with that which is missing from a situation. Their own standards are the deciding factor here: even when the world calls things good enough, type 1 may still be dissatisfied because he is of the opinion that it ought to have been better. Everything can be improved in the type 1 world! This is how they unconsciously make sure they remain in close contact with their own imperfection, the very thing they would do anything to keep away from.

***If you don't meet your own standards, then you are doing things wrong and are imperfect.***

Under all circumstances, type 1 must avoid falling short of his own standards. That's hard work, especially if you have a standard for everything. Type 1 people practically work a full-time job keeping from making mistakes and making sure they don't fail to meet their standards. Their internal critic works overtime preventing slip-ups and errors, and is never afraid to point out to others their imperfections. Type 1's clear opinions about how things ought to be often place him in the position of role model. He doesn't just strive to live by his own standards; he motivates others to do the same. People who like to cut corners, don't uphold agreements, or those who generally don't meet type 1's standards can count on his correction. Critical of others as he may be, he is even more critical of himself. However, type 1 doesn't easily entrust responsibility to others, because if things are done his way, at least they are done properly. Again, the word 'properly' is interchangeable with 'according to his standard'. Naturally, all type 1 people have their own specific standards. For example, one particular type 1 friend of mine considers it irresponsible for a mother to work after having children. Another type 1 friend holds the exact opposite to be true: she believes it an outrage that in this day and age, there are still stay-at-home mothers who don't have careers. Both these women are type 1 people, yet their standards couldn't be more different. What they have in common is their motivation: both live and breathe their own strict standards 24/7. There is only one standard that all type 1 people agree on wholeheartedly: perfect people shouldn't be furious, they should be self-contained.

***If you are irritated, then you must always remain self-contained.***

Put yourself in the following position: each day you are irritated no end by all the imperfection in yourself and the world, and on top of that, your unconscious standard is that you should always contain your anger. It's quite a challenge! Often, all that pent up irritation and anger becomes visible to others. It may also be transformed into an urge to improve and correct. The irritation is what drives type 1 to go and perfect matters. These are all transformed reactions of anger. The anger is repressed and practically every impulsive and instinctive reaction is first presented to something of a 'standards bureau': "Is this reaction passable according to the standard? Can it be expressed?"

As expected when irritation and anger are systematically contained, type 1's reserves fill up over time. At a certain point the dam will burst, and type 1 is shown to be human after all. He becomes furious and unleashes his anger. This is not part of the plan. Anger is, after all, a sign of imperfection, the very thing type 1 wishes to avoid. It's outside his comfort zone. So his unconscious coach springs into action and motivates him to do what he does best: improving himself! While he is at it, he will correct the world around him as well. This is his arena, making everything fit his standards and values. It's the safest way to be. That's how type 1 unconsciously keeps his vicious cycle going, and how his unconscious coach works overtime to keep him in his comfort zone.

## WELCOME TO THE WORLD OF TYPE 2

### DON'T DO IT FOR ME, DO IT FOR YOURSELF!

***If I contribute to the happiness of others 24/7, then I will be needed and deserve their love. I will never be left empty-handed and will never fall short. Then I will be able to survive safely.***

Imagine always and immediately sensing what it is that others need. Imagine believing whole-heartedly that you are the one that can make a difference in people's lives, believing that you can fulfil those needs. Type 2 people do not only believe this: their whole existence depends on it. A type 2's autopilot spends all day, every day, focused on the needs of others. This helps him make sure they are never lacking in anything. The ultimate reward is the delicious feeling that he is important to others: pride.

Pride is the motor of the type 2 person; it motivates him to concern himself 24/7 with the requirements of others. It also happens to be his greatest strength. He possess an enormous drive to contribute to the lives of others; to help them draw the best from themselves and the situation they're in. Type 2 people want others to have the best they can; suppressing their own needs in the process is second nature.

***If you recognise a need in someone, then you must either fulfil it or, at the very least, contribute something.***

Being needed, that's the name of the game. Type 2's own needs are somewhat lower on the list of priorities; the recognition that comes with making a positive difference is a reward in itself. A thoughtful compliment, a pat on the shoulder, making others feels good, is what type 2 people are made for. They will think along with you, offer their help, and share tips and advice; all without asking. None of this seems to be any trouble for type 2, and unconsciously it gives him the positive feeling that he is contributing. Type 2 people automatically scan for what others need so they can be necessary to them and fill the shortages in their lives. There isn't much good in the world they wouldn't wish on others. By giving others what they need, type 2 people hope to earn the love, recognition and appreciation they themselves desire. It's the perfect trade-off. I give you what you need, and in return I receive the recognition that I am important to you, perhaps even indispensable. This gives type 2 his right to exist. The idea that type 2 could receive love without contributing is unimaginable.

***If you make a difference in the lives of others, then you deserve appreciation and love.***

Give before you receive, that's the motto; and even then receiving is a tricky thing. When type 2 receives, he often feels indebted to others. To him, it's equivalent to coming up short. That makes it time to give back; quickly, before others start paying attention to what he needs instead. It isn't as if type 2 doesn't consider himself important; he does. He just keeps his own needs safely tucked away in contact with others. It's difficult for type 2 to bear others making an effort for him. He can't stand the idea that they would do, or refrain from doing, something for his sake, particularly at their own expense. Type 2 people take the wishes and desires of others into account at all times, but conversely, they would do anything to keep from being needy. For type 2, 'being needy' means not being there for others and (even worse!) having to ask them to do something for you. In type 2's mind, this is the same as selling the other person short. Unfortunately, by always giving more than they receive, a type 2 keeps others in his debt. This keeps relationships vertical and he ends up selling the other person short.

***If you need something from someone, then you are in their debt and you come up short.***

When in contact with others, type 2 unconsciously suppresses his needs and desires. Rather than focusing on his own needs, he aims all his attention towards those of others. It's simply impossible for him, at that time, to get in touch with what he wants. Instead, type 2 scans what those around him want, and makes sure everyone gets their share. It isn't until later, or when he is alone, that he can get in touch with what he has suppressed, with what he truly needs and wants. Goal-oriented as they are, type 2 people go after the desires they have identified with zeal; but never at the expense of others. In fact, if it's at all possible, his desires should really benefit others as well. For example, if type 2 feels like going to the beach, that could be fortunate because it gives him a chance to stop by his mother who lives nearby. He just needs to leave his daughter at home for a bit, but she has a friend visiting, so that should be fine. Quickly, all needs are scanned; only then can type 2 execute his plans. He decides to visit his mother first; that was more convenient for her. Halfway through his second cup of tea he gets a phone call from his darling daughter. She has had an argument with her friend and is in tears. That's it for type 2's walk on the beach. He heads home; he is needed. An hour in the car each way, an hour and a half of tea with mum, and drying his daughters tears at home. At the end of the day everyone is pampered and taken care of. His mother calls, letting him know she was so happy with his visit and his daughter is back to her radiant self. She is out with a different friend by now. Unconsciously, type 2 always asks, who needs me the most? Where can I contribute? In practice this means easily suppressing his own needs, and that relaxing walks on the beach lose out...

***If you suppress what you want, then you can contribute more to others.***

Nobody is allowed lack anything; you must always be available to the important people around you. Type 2 is generous, big-hearted, and giving, but also selective. He aims his attentions towards a select group of people close to him. He will walk through fire for them and, if necessary, completely discount himself. Type 2 doesn't see it that way, however; he simply cannot help contributing. What he does feel is exhaustion, particularly after giving too much of himself, and resentment over doing so much for others and getting so little in return. That's type 2's secret wish: that others, without his asking, will finally sense what *he* needs. Not that he'd get very far with that; receiving isn't his strongest point.

A resentful mood usually doesn't last very long; type 2 is a positive thinker who doesn't want to bother others with his troubles. That would, after all, mean he was needy. It's outside his comfort zone. So, his unconscious coach springs into action and motivates him to do what he does best: being needed instead of needing anything for himself. This is his arena: being important to others and contributing to their happiness. It's the safest way to be. That's how type 2 unconsciously keeps his vicious cycle going, and how his unconscious coach works overtime to keep him in his comfort zone.

## WELCOME TO THE WORLD OF TYPE 3

### CHECK!

***If I deliver and focus on the world of achievements 27/4, then I will achieve my goals and be successful. I will not have to experience my failure. Then I will be able to survive safely.***

Imagine being convinced that who you are is what you do. Imagine only being worthwhile when you perform well, when you achieve things. The opposite is also true: if you do nothing, you're worth nothing. In fact, doing nothing can be a life threatening condition, because who *are* you, when you do nothing at all? So, you make sure you do as much as possible. It's convenient, when taking action, to focus on the world of achievements; the outside world, that is. That's where you can score, where you can achieve goals. This means putting things out there, where everyone can witness them, things that contribute to a positive reputation. For a type 3 person, everything is achievable. As long as you are willing to put in the effort, everything will go your way: that's what type 3 believes more than anything. If you want it, you can do it. By ignoring everything outside the world of achievements, everything that can't be turned into a success, type 3 deceives himself and those around him. This form of deceit is the motor of type 3: it motivates him to focus his energy 24/7 onto the outside world. It also happens to be his greatest strength: an enormous drive to accomplish many things. Without being distracted by negative emotions and other obstacles, type 3 always keeps going for new targets.

***If you make an effort, then everything is achievable and you will accomplish your goals.***

Under all circumstances, type 3 wants to achieve his goals. Achieving a great deal, for him, is the same as being worth a great deal. His identity is derived from his accomplishments and he particularly wants to do well in the eyes of others. This is how he hopes to win acknowledgement and appreciation. Type 3 people are good at reaching goals, and want to check as many of them off as possible in a day. People who want to tick off lots of items on their list are usually really good at setting achievable goals for themselves, goals that almost guarantee success, and type 3 is no exception. With every instance, type 3 unconsciously asks the question, "Will this bring me closer to my goal?" Because, unconsciously, type 3 is convinced he is what he achieves, he tends to be perpetually busy and loves to do things. The more he achieves, the better he feels. He likes to think positively, avoids negative emotions (obstacles on the way to his target) and has a love of efficiency. Type 3 is characterised by a fast pace of life. This makes sense, because achieving ten goals will always be more rewarding that achieving five, so there is no time to lose. The challenge is to check off as many goals as possible, and with every tick his self-esteem increases.

***If you set achievable targets, then you will achieve success faster and you will be able to check off more goals.***

At any cost, type 3 wants to prevent missing a previously set target, or otherwise risking damage to his reputation. His image in the eyes of others is what counts, after all. This image needs to be positive. Failure is not an option. For type 3, failure is a personal defeat. Under no circumstances does type 3 want the image of being unsuccessful so he is cautious when setting his targets. Short-term goals are preferred; they carry fewer risks than long-term ones. He organises popular support, is a natural networker, and does anything to create a path of least resistance toward his goal. If, despite all type 3's preparations, failure threatens, then the goal is subtly adjusted along the way, or it just disappears at the bottom of a busy agenda. If failure truly can't be avoided, type 3 would prefer to call it a 'learning experience', a necessary stop on the way to success.

***If you don't achieve your goals, then you fail.***

Type 3 people are generally comfortable socially. They are flexible and easily identify with others. Like a chameleon, they take on the colour of their surroundings. A type 3 person will just as easily socialise with a politician as with a blue-collar worker. If he is on a roll, he might just take on their accents to boot. Type 3's autopilot constantly scans his surroundings so he can anticipate what's expected of him. He is a master of social adaptation. There is, of course, an unconscious motive for this. By taking on the colour of his surroundings, type 3 chooses the kind of behaviour that will trigger least resistance, and most success in that situation. Type 3 chooses the behaviour that gets him to his goal the fastest.

***If you identify with others or your surroundings, then you reach your goals faster.***

Opposition isn't useful for type 3. It just causes delays. He derives his sense of self-worth from his accomplishments and reputation, and that's also where his identity comes from. He is what he accomplishes. He is his reputation, his image. This is why he often talks about his achievements, about doing things. He does this in a seemingly casual way, making them sound even more impressive. Type 3 accomplishes a lot, with seemingly very little effort.

With his social flexibility, type 3 hopes to avoid bumps in the road to his target. Unfortunately, in doing so, he runs the risk of disappearing like a chameleon himself, of having very little identity of his own. His breakneck pace, while rushing him towards his goals, prevents him from spending a lot of time on his interior world. Furthermore, his tendency to forget about the process, rather than the goal, can cause him to lose people on the way. All this, as well as his chameleon-like behaviour, can trigger resistance. Who is he really? Resistance to a type 3 person is the same as failure. If his behaviour and accomplishments are not appreciated, then what is left of him? That's exactly what type 3 wants to avoid. It's outside his comfort zone, and so, his unconscious coach springs into action and motivates him to do what he does best, focusing on the world of achievements, his arena. There he can accomplish new goals and succeed. It's the safest way to be. That's how type 3 unconsciously keeps his vicious cycle going, and how his unconscious coach works overtime to keep him in his comfort zone.

## WELCOME TO THE WORLD OF TYPE 4

### I BEG TO DIFFER...

***If I follow my feelings and am authentic 24/7, then I will genuinely be myself. I will not have to connect with others and I will not be rejected. Then I can survive safely.***

Imagine having the tendency to constantly compare yourself negatively to others. Imagine having the feeling that something is missing in you that others seem to have naturally. Imagine perpetually feeling like an outsider, like you don't quite fit in. The type 4 person constantly senses what is missing from the world, from life, and specifically from himself. The latter is mostly experienced in contact with others. They possess something he doesn't. Life is just easier for others, things are always extra difficult for him. It seems as if they don't find it so hard to conform, whereas he is always in touch with what isn't there. He always knows what's missing. This is why it's difficult for type 4 to conform with others. He often feels misunderstood and finds it equally challenging to understand other people. Being in connection with another person feels dangerous to him. He might long for it, but it is particularly in contact with others that type 4 feels envy. They have something he doesn't have. This form of envy is the motor of the type 4 person: it motivates him to constantly compare himself negatively to others and to keep searching for that which is missing from himself. It also happens to be his greatest strength: an enormous drive to genuinely be himself; he will do anything for that. Type 4 people also motivate those around them to stay genuine and authentic.

***If you compare yourself to others, then you feel that something is missing in yourself.***

It is as difficult for type 4 to identify with others as it is easy for type 3. He will always see the differences between himself and the other person, and will always find confirmation that he is different from others. The fear of rejection is ever present. This is why type 4 prefers to identify with himself instead; it's a lot safer. In fact, his highest purpose is to truly be himself. How do you do that? By identifying with your feelings. Nothing is more real, more authentic, than your feelings, which is why type 4 takes them very seriously. Type 4 people constantly study their feelings and their interior world. But when can you trust them? Just a minute ago, you felt sad thinking of your father, now you feel anger, and last night you felt sympathy. Which of these feelings should you take seriously? Welcome to the world of type 4. He spends all day analysing and intensifying his feelings. After all, his feelings make him unique. Type 4 tends to conflate intensity and authenticity. The more intensely he experiences things, the more authentic they are to him. This gives him a tendency to intensify and dramatise his emotions. The more he feels, the more he lives, the more authentic he is! Type 4 is what he feels.

***If you are truly yourself and live by your feelings, then you are authentic.***

In practice, being yourself often means being unlike the rest, and that is exactly what type 4 unconsciously aims for. In all circumstances, he wants to prevent himself from becoming another face in the crowd. Type 4 wants to avoid being just as everyday, as mediocre, as those around him. Particularly, he wants to avoid being lumped into the same category with them. Of course, he has an unconscious investment in this system. Type 4 is always afraid of being exposed or being found wanting, when he is compared to others. Type 4 assumes that when he is judged by the same standard as others, he will compare negatively. Therefore he avoids any situation where he might be compared. Mediocrity, for type 4, also includes everything boring, routine, everything that doesn't lead to intense feelings. Dullness, ruts and superficiality; type 4 would rather stay away. He is what he feels, after all. That's where his identity is drawn from. This means it's important for him to always stay in close contact with his feelings, to intensify them where necessary and to avoid mediocrity.

*If you are just like others, then you will be rejected.*

In order to avoid looking like the rest, type 4 makes sure he is always be slightly distinguished from them. That's safe, because it is in connection with others that rejection happens. It's better to stay one step ahead. Like anyone else, type 4 longs for connection, but his fear of rejection makes it difficult for him to connect to others; it feels like conforming. This happens unconsciously: when everyone else says yes, type 4 will have the urge to say no. He is acutely aware of the difference between himself and the other person. Unconsciously he always checks whether he feels the same way as others do, which is rarely the case. Type 4 always sees things slightly differently. He knows, be it unconsciously, that conforming with others is dangerous and should be avoided at all times. Being yourself, for type 4, is the same as being different. Being unique, unlike the rest is safe; you can't be rejected that way.

*If you set yourself apart, then you will not be rejected.*

Attraction and rejection; connecting and detachment, this is the pattern of type 4's relationships. He will always manage to set himself apart by explicitly drawing attention to himself or to stand out by not participating at all. His strategy of non-connection presents itself in the form of always being a little bit different from the rest. It's also visible in type 4's never conforming without question, and can be seen in his holding a mirror up to people who he thinks are playing games, or pretending to be better than they are. Type 4 is allergic to inauthentic behaviour like that. Because he always wants to be authentic himself, he will never hide his annoyance over these matters and is quick to reject others. This often results in his own rejection.

Being rejected confirms the sensitive type 4 person's own worldview: you see, when I am myself, I will be rejected. This is exactly what he has been trying to avoid. It is outside his comfort zone, so his unconscious coach springs into action and motivates him to do what he does best, focusing on his feelings and distinguishing between himself and others. This is his arena, where he can truly be himself. It's the safest way to be. That's how type 4 unconsciously keeps his vicious cycle going, and how his unconscious coach works overtime to keep him in his comfort zone.

## WELCOME TO THE WORLD OF TYPE 5

### DO NOT DISTURB!

***If I focus on the objective world and remain reasonable 24/7, then I will not become dependent on the subjective and emotional world. Then I can survive safely.***

Imagine being convinced of the fact that there is never enough of everything you need in the world. There is a shortage of time, money, energy, knowledge and space. You have to be somewhat frugal with these things, because you need to have enough of them in order to survive. Type 5 is convinced of this, and for that reason he strives not to become too dependent on people and emotions. In fact, people *are* emotions, which makes them unreasonable by definition. People cost time and energy, and perhaps even money and space. Type 5's highest goal is to be independent and self-supporting. In order to achieve this he has to be reasonable and well informed at all times. This realisation is what feeds type 5's greed: his motor. Greed motivates him to always make sure he has enough of everything he needs to support himself. It also happens to be his greatest strength: an enormous drive to be independent. For a type 5 this means being well informed and self-reliant. He always strives for objectivity and reason and invites those around him to do the same.

***If you have enough of everything, then you can be self-supporting and independent.***

Under all circumstances, type 5 wants to be someone who understands how things work in this world. Collecting knowledge has the highest priority. The better you understand the world, the easier it is to support yourself. If you know how to fix a bicycle tyre yourself, you won't have to ask anyone for help. That means you won't have to let any people, any emotions, in. Type 5 people are excellent observers and spend all day collecting information. In doing so type 5 focuses his attention on the objective, observable world. He focuses on supported facts, things that are objectively demonstrable, those he can work with. Type 5 aims to be one hundred percent informed. If you know everything there is to know about something, there are no exceptions and everything will be verifiably correct. That's a safe feeling; in fact, it is the epitome of objectivity! But when do you ever know you have a hundred percent of the information? Rarely! This is why type 5 always feels like he is missing information. Only when he has all the information can he make a decision, and that can take a while. If type 5 does come up with an opinion it will always be well supported by facts, by knowledge, not by feelings. By doing this, type 5 tries unconsciously to make sure his opinion doesn't trigger any emotions in others. He assumes that when his conclusions are based on facts, others will see their reason and they won't respond emotionally to them. Type 5 is always prepared to revise his opinion when new information becomes available. He is curious, always wants to know more and likes to enter into debate to that effect. He asks 'why' a lot and his feeling that information is missing makes him insatiable in that respect. Type 5 wants to know more. More knowledge equals more independence.

***If you understand how something works, then you can remain independent, objective and reasonable.***

Type 5 is often more of an observer than a participant in life. There is so much to see, hear and observe if you enjoy collecting knowledge. Many type 5 people can even observe themselves observing the world, as if from a distance. Studying the world has another benefit: it creates a safe distance and keeps you away from people and too many emotions. Under all circumstances, type 5 wants to avoid becoming dependent on emotions, his own, and those of others. Before you know it, you can be overwhelmed by emotions, and then where will you be? Emotions cost time and energy, and there isn't much type 5 can do with them. He always needs more time to think and feels out of his depth when things get too emotional. In type 5's experience, things easily become too emotional. Anything that's not objective and factual, type 5 experiences as subjective and emotional. Trusting your instincts, letting others come too close and investigating your interior world: these things are tricky for type 5; he sees them as a threat to his independence. By staying reasonable and logical he hopes to keep intense emotions out. Unfortunately, this doesn't always work in practice. His chilly, impassive (reasonable) demeanour can trigger all sorts of emotions in others. It's often hard for others to see what type 5 is going through, what he really thinks and feels. Instead of being guided by those unreasonable emotions, type 5 always wants to decide wisely. People that are this afraid of emotions must be incredibly sensitive. Despite this, type 5's constant rationality can make him seem distant and cold, even as his feelings are building up inside. When those feelings come out it's often unexpected, and a bit clumsy. After all, type 5 doesn't have much experience expressing his emotions.

***If you want to be independent, then you must avoid emotions and subjectivity.***

When type 5 is overwhelmed by emotions, his own or those of others, he withdraws. That's his automatic response when he is confronted with irrationality, when he threatens to lose his sense of perspective, when his emotions become too much for him or when his head becomes overfull with information. Note that type 5 hardly filters information at all, he registers everything. He does this because that extra information could always come in handy, and, moreover, it also satisfies his greed. Knowing a lot feels good, and is addictive. As a result, type 5 often feels swamped with information and emotions. That's when he withdraws for a moment to sort out his mind. Sometimes it is a physical withdrawal: sitting in another room, going for a drive in his car, or going to the gym. But type 5 is also versed in the art of being absently present. He may restore order in his brain, even in the company of others. He can withdraw into his own mind, being there, but also being elsewhere. Type 5 can behave appropriately on the surface, while he orders and processes the emotions and information he has collected.

***If you want to recharge, then you need to withdraw.***

Type 5's withdrawal behaviour can, in itself, provoke responses as well. Where people shield themselves, they create intruders. This is also a common complaint among type 5 people: that others can be so intrusive, when type 5 wishes for time and space to himself. The idea that he creates this situation himself, by keeping the world out so systematically, often doesn't enter type 5's mind. In any case, it's a full-time job for type 5, keeping those intrusive emotional people out. All this when he is so aware that everything is finite, that he needs to be careful with his time and energy lest they run out.

By staying reasonable and neutral, type 5 hopes to prevent others from becoming too emotional and irrational. On top of that, the objective is to keep people at a safe distance. If they get too close, they might ask about his subjective experience of things, or even about his feelings. That's way too invasive for type 5, and it costs him too much energy. He doesn't feel capable of managing situations like that; they threaten his independence. That's exactly what type 5 wants to avoid; it's outside his comfort zone. So his unconscious coach springs into action and motivates him to do what he does best: focusing on the outside world and collecting knowledge. Being objective and reasonable: that's his arena. This is where he can go back to being independent and where he can support himself. That's how type 5 unconsciously keeps his vicious cycle going, and how his unconscious coach works overtime to keep him in his comfort zone.

## WELCOME TO THE WORLD OF TYPE 6

### YES, BUT...

***If I anticipate other people's expectations and am loyal 24/7, then I will be less insecure and I will not have to rely on myself. Then I can survive safely.***

Imagine constantly feeling a certain type of unrest. You can't quite explain why, but you are always somewhat nervous and tense, as if you need to be alert, prepared for things to go wrong. That is what all type 6 people realise: you can never just assume things will go right. If, on top of that, you are someone who has a hard time trusting in himself, it makes sense that you would be extra nervous and fearful most of the time. This fear is the motor of type 6. It's a good guide for pointing out all the dangers in life. It also motivates type 6 to organise his security outside himself. Type 6 does this by being a hard worker, because you can't feel as much uncertainty when you're busy, and by anticipating the expectations of others. This also happens to be type 6's greatest strength: an enormous drive to connect with his surroundings. He is loyal to others and strives for equality: everyone is equally important, so why stand out?

***If you are afraid or insecure, then you must always trust in others and be loyal to them.***

It's difficult for type 6 to trust in his own authority. He is chronically insecure and experiences a lot of doubt. This is why he would rather trust in others, scan his environment for expectations, and meet them where possible. Type 6 must avoid doing anything wrong, because if you expose yourself by making mistakes others may just abandon you. Relying on others for your own self-confidence isn't a desirable situation. Others are supposed to give type 6 affirmation and reassurance, things he isn't very good at giving himself. This is how type 6 unknowingly gives other people a lot of power over him, and why he adapts to them so easily. It makes him a loyal team player, one who often puts aside his own interests for the benefit of the group. Type 6 likes to prepare as well as possible in order to be ready for any unexpected situations. He doesn't make a decision until all contingency plans and worst-case scenarios are thought through as much as possible. Type 6 often anticipates problems ahead, which is a quality that helps him tackle dangerous situations and threats up front. He strives to create security and be trustworthy. Type 6 people tend to realise quite early on that the bigger they are, the harder they fall, and choose instead for safe behaviour. In practice, this often means type 6 is dutiful, caring and modest.

***If you anticipate the expectations of others, then that gives you guidance and structure.***

Under all circumstances, type 6 must prevent falling prey to his internal insecurities. His uncertainty is troublesome, but it has a great advantage: while you are in doubt, you are unclear, and you don't have to profile yourself. While you are in doubt you may still decide either way, and you can still be flexible and go along with your surroundings. It's a safe strategy. Type 6 doesn't just doubt himself, his 'yes, but...' strategy will call into question everything you say as well. This, at least, ensures he isn't the only one who is insecure. Taking a stand or being conspicuous, to a type 6, means sticking your neck out. He is convinced this can't end well and prefers to avoid it at any cost. This is why he always remains a little bit vague and unclear, and why he looks for clarity and guidance outside himself. Type 6 is most at home around solid agreements and clear expectations. If things still end up going wrong, then at least it won't be his fault. Consciously, of course, type 6 doesn't want to be ruled by doubt and uncertainty, but unconsciously he benefits from it. He tends to look for a lot of affirmation outside himself; a process that he prefers to call 'asking for clarification'.

***If you question everything, then you will feel less insecure. Being conspicuous = scary***

Fear is an unpleasant sensation. It's even less enjoyable when you don't know where it comes from, or why you are feeling agitated and restless. It helps to be able to explain the disquiet, to look around you to find its cause. This is how type 6 projects his fear and insecurity: of course you have to be alert, people can't be trusted, the world is unsafe and you never know when someone will stick by his word. All these explanations help type 6 unconsciously keep his fear alive. As long as he finds causes for his fear in the outside world, he will not have to acknowledge that it's part of himself. Projection is type 6's *middle name.* He often applies it to the future as well, to stay ahead of danger, seeing trouble ahead, thinking through problem scenarios: these are all forms of projection. All this helps him diminish the fear, but also to feed it.

***If you imagine or expect everything that might go wrong, then things can only turn out better.***

Those who only see risks, work with caution. Type 6 often encourages himself to be fearful by only seeing those things that may go wrong. The constant asking of questions also breeds uncertainty, even if you need the answers to achieve clarity. After all, every question forces you into contact with your own uncertainty, which often ends up creating more of it. One person might tell you this, the other, that. Which answer can you trust? What will happen when the authority you are loyal to turns out to be untrustworthy? The bottom would drop out of your world.

By projecting, by focusing on everything that might go wrong, type 6 tends to organise his own unrest. Even thought this is exactly the feeling of insecurity and fear that he wants to avoid. It's outside his comfort zone. So his unconscious coach springs into action and motivates him to do what he does best: searching for certainty outside himself, and being loyal to others. This is his arena. It's where he can go back to anticipating expectations, and where he doesn't have to rely on himself. It's the safest way to be. That's how type 6 unconsciously keeps his vicious cycle going, and how his unconscious coach works overtime to keep him in his comfort zone.

## WELCOME TO THE WORLD OF TYPE 7

### CAN I HAVE SOME MORE?

***If I make sure my life is enjoyable by organising lots of experiences 24/7, then I will not have to face my own pain and limitations. Then I can survive safely.***

Imagine realising time and again that life is way too short to do everything you want to. Also imagine being determined to achieve happiness by not missing one bit of everything amazing that life has to offer. That must lead to a certain amount of panic. It makes you realise that, as a human being, you are limited. Not only do you have a limited amount of time on earth, much of it is filled with things that you don't feel like doing in the least. It's unfortunate, because that's the one thing type 7 wants to avoid at all costs: limitations. Instead, he wants to experience as much as possible of all the great things in life, he doesn't want to miss a thing. This is why he organises as many pleasurable experiences as possible. The more, the better! The motor of type 7 is excess. It motivates him to get as many kicks, to find as much distraction, stimulation and as many fun experiences in life as possible. This also happens to be type 7's greatest strength: an enormously enthusiastic and optimistic attitude to life, and the quality of keeping things light and drawing others into their enjoyment. After all, life is meant to be enjoyed!

***If you want to be happy, then you need to organise many pleasurable experiences and make sure you are never limited.***

At all times, type 7 wants to be in touch with the enjoyable side of life. As far as he is concerned, the possibilities are endless. Unconsciously, he realises that 'not being difficult' is the key to happiness. Always look on the bright side is his motto. Type 7 cruises through life as breezily as possible. He would rather not tie himself down too much, and prefers to be able to impulsively go where he wants. Freedom is the most important thing for type 7. He is good at thinking of possibilities and focusing on the future. Everything is possible in the future; there are no limits. Type 7 loves to make new plans, he loves to fantasise about all the fun things he might do in life. These plans often don't even need to be executed. The mental pleasure that type 7 people derive from just making them is enough. The world is full of limitations, but everything is possible inside your mind. That's where you can make the most beautiful journeys, the most romantic encounters, and where you can always move freely.

***If you keep things light, then they will stay fun and enjoyable.***

In all circumstances, type 7 wants to prevent life from becoming too heavy and depressing. This is why he tends to avoid painful situations. He organises a lot of distraction to keep away from his own pain and difficulties. Type 7 can spot pain and sorrow a mile away; that's how afraid he is of it. He avoids it like the plague, an analogy which characterises the way he experiences it rather well. However, sometimes type 7 will go looking for pain on purpose, because being close to it can feel good. He is also an expert at relieving pain in others and derives pleasurable confirmation from doing so. Type 7 is easily upset, however, when he becomes the victim of painful circumstances himself. He likes to have things his way, and is quickly frustrated when he can't get what he wants. The opposite of excess is limitation; the former is fun, the latter is horror. Being tempered or limited is painful and type 7 seeks to steer clear of it at all costs. When called upon to delay gratification, type 7 is easily distracted; he will soon direct his attentions elsewhere. In fact, type 7 always does this when things around him stop being entertaining; as quickly as possible, he switches over to something more exciting. The worst kind of criticism is to tell him that he isn't fun to spend time with; he will do anything to be just the opposite. Being good company is so important to him because type 7 assumes others will be more fun, and less difficult, when you are. So if this hasn't worked out, that's hard for him to handle. If people are being difficult, type 7 will try to cheer them up. If that doesn't work, he probably has somewhere else he needs to be. Type 7 is no stranger to the flight response.

***If you let your pain in, then life becomes hard and you limit yourself.***

In order not to feel the painful and unpleasant side of life, type 7 will rationalise away anything remotely distressing. He tends to look for logical explanations for his pain, and will always try to put a positive spin on things. "Ok, so the divorce wasn't great, but at least it opened up some new perspectives." Type 7 will always try to look at new opportunities and possibilities, anything to deny the constraints of life. He teaches himself to always stay away from pessimism, to put a positive spin on every misfortune, all in order to keep things cheerful. He is a master of letting go, moving on, and distracting himself by transferring his attentions away from pain onto something else. His reflex reaction is to rationalise all pain away. It happens faster than light.

***If you rationalise the pain away, then you can stay optimistic.***

Type 7's lightness is his charm, but also his pitfall. It gives him the tendency not to take life very seriously. This inclines him towards a certain superficiality. Imagine taking life seriously though; you might have to start paying attention to its downsides, its sadness and disappointments. That's not how type 7 imagined things would be; life was supposed to be fun. This is why his level of commitment is often low: he stays as long as he is having a good time. If something excites type 7, he generally cannot get enough; he will crave excessive amounts of it. Unfortunately, it's more in his nature to hop from one fascination to the next, either physically or in his imagination. He does this in the hope of keeping things interesting, but it often leads to a lack of satisfaction. He ends up always racing towards something else instead of enjoying the moment. His life becomes flighty and always headed for the future. Type 7 unconsciously creates a growing emptiness inside himself, one that needs an increasing amount of stimulation to be sated. If you rush between three parties in one night because you don't want to miss a single one, you might end up never really being present at any of them. This, in the end, still feels unsatisfying and painful.

It's exactly this pain which type 7 seeks to hide from. It's outside his comfort zone. That's when his unconscious coach springs into action and motivates him to do what he does best: arranging lots of different stimuli and experiences, devising new plans, his arena. This allows him to stay closely in touch with the happy side of life. It's the safest way to be. That's how type 7 unconsciously keeps his vicious cycle going, and how his unconscious coach works overtime to keep him in his comfort zone.

## WELCOME TO THE WORLD OF TYPE 8

### I'LL DO IT MYSELF!

***If I pull the strings 24/7, then I can make the decisions and keep control over my life. I will not have to allow others to influence me. Then I can survive safely.***

Imagine clearly believing that you are on your own in life; you are the only one who can make things happen for yourself. Trusting in others is dangerous business. Other people may abuse their power and set you back. This is the base fear of the type 8 person, and that's why he has unconsciously decided to always stay in charge of his own life. He trusts primarily in himself. In order to do this, you need to feel energised and powerful. Type 8 knows this very well. His motor is lust for life, anything that boosts his energy. This is what motivates him, what gets him out of bed in the morning. In everything he does, type 8 unconsciously asks the following question: will this give me energy? If the answer is yes, he moves full steam ahead. If the answer is no, however, type 8 will not act at all. Type 8 people are addicted to everything that generates energy (lust for life), which could mean a variety of things. Anything between good food, physical activity and social contacts could be an energiser for him. This also happens to be his greatest strength: an enormous drive to feel his own strength, and to stimulate others to be in touch with theirs. Nonsense and half-heartedness are strictly avoided. Clarity and directness are type 8's qualities. What you see is what you get.

***If you only commit to things that boost your energy, then you will stay powerful.***

At all times, the type 8 person wants to feel in touch with his own strength. Being strong, that's the main goal, because otherwise you won't last long in this world. That makes it important to hold on to the reins at all times, because only then can you decide for yourself. It's not that type 8 wants to dominate others, even though it might seem that way sometimes. He must stay in charge because otherwise others might dominate him. It's tricky: when others are in charge you never know if things will turn out ok. Trusting others is no easy feat for this personality type. Surrender is nearly impossible. As long as you are the one pulling the strings, you are in control of your own life. This is why you have to be strong, why you mustn't complain or be weak, why you must never let anyone deflate you. Type 8 is virtually allergic to those who victimise themselves. Those who have been truly victimised, however, will meet strong support from him. The powerful type 8 person loves to take vulnerable people into his protection; it makes him feel even stronger. He isn't someone to choose the path of least resistance; only when he has fought for something does type 8 consider it worth his wile. Struggling, after all, is for the strong.

***Only if you are strong will you have control of the reins and can you decide for yourself.***

Under all circumstances, type 8 must prevent others from influencing what happens in his life. He doesn't trust that at all, it makes him weak and vulnerable. You never know, after all, what other people might do with their power over you. There is always a danger of abuse. The fear of being put at a disadvantage is great in type 8. He is cautious in that respect. He wants to avoid being vulnerable. For a type 8 person, vulnerability is feeling like he doesn't control his own life and that, therefore, others will. For him, having others decide means being out of control; it's a dangerous situation. In many ways, type 8 is the opposite of type 6. A type 6 person feels safe as long as he can place his trust in others; type 8 feels safe when he can trust only himself. Type 6 is heavily invested in doubt; type 8 hates it. For him, life is black and white; grey is not an option. If you are at all unclear, others will determine things for you. That must be avoided. Type 8 needs to keep influence from others at arm's length at all times. The influence of his own negative emotions is treated similarly: they can sap your strength, another thing to be avoided.

***If you allow things to influence you, then you are vulnerable.***

In order to prevent things from having a negative influence on him, type 8 unconsciously denies everything that blocks him from feeling strong. "Don't be silly, I don't have back problems; I'm just a bit sore from my workout." Crying is for wimps, and so type 8 just denies anything that bothers him. Physical limitations to his strength, such as illness, injury and his pain threshold in general, are ignored as long as possible. He does the same for mental limitations. Being bothered by something or someone, for type 8, is the same as allowing them to control him. He must prevent that from happening; he is too afraid of being disadvantaged when others make the decisions. Even scarier is the idea of his power being in some way drained when he allows something to affect him. This is the reason type 8 isn't often bothered by things. When others complain about him, he prefers to act unaffected: "Well, that's your problem then..." Type 8 people regularly overexert themselves because they have trouble admitting that they too, have their weaknesses. These are not allowed; they threaten type 8's ideal, strong and powerful self-image.

***When you feel that something or someone is sapping your strength, then you deny it.***

There is no limit to type 8's autonomy; a human being is never a victim. No matter what, a person decides his own destiny. That's the worldview of type 8. His strategy is to decide everything for himself, and to leave little influence to others. This strategy is taxing over time. Type 8 runs the risk of overestimating the limits of what he can bear. He risks denying for too long that he is only human, that sometimes even he is bothered by pain, fear, sadness and other people's reactions.

Type 8's propensity to overestimate his limits gives him a tendency to exceed them and to overtax himself. This makes him vulnerable and unable to decide for himself. This is exactly what he was trying to avoid. It's outside his comfort zone. So his unconscious coach springs into action and motivates him to do what he does best: taking hold of the reins and being in charge, his arena. This way, he can keep out all negative influence and stay strong and powerful. It's the safest way to be. That's how type 8 unconsciously keeps his vicious cycle going, and how his unconscious coach works overtime to keep him in his comfort zone.

## WELCOME TO THE WORLD OF TYPE 9

### IT'S NO BIG DEAL!

***If I protect the peace and harmony and keep my opinions to myself 24/7, then I will not cause any conflicts and will not have to feel my own agitation. Then I can survive safely.***

Imagine always wanting to keep everything peaceful and harmonious, because that's how you like your surroundings. If you did, it would be wise if you didn't make yourself too important, if you didn't share too many opinions. You will not trigger much opposition that way, and you won't disturb the peace. At least, that's what type 9 thinks. Sloth is his motor; it motivates him not to act. Every action, after all, may cause waves in the water. It's better not to stand out too much, to stay relaxed and go with the flow. It also happens to be type 9's greatest strength: an enormous capacity to keep the peace and maintain a good atmosphere. Type 9 is an expert at giving others the space they need, and making sure everyone is heard and acknowledged. For himself he prefers a modest background position.

***If you stand out or distinguish yourself, then you create a disturbance.***

Under all circumstances, type 9 wants to keep the peace. The best way to do this is to make sure you are always contented. Type 9 is convinced contented people make few demands and provoke few negative reactions and disturbances. How do you make sure you are always satisfied with life? It's simple: don't put too much importance on yourself. While you're at it, you might as well decide that nothing is really important enough to get worked up about. Don't kick up a fuss, don't put yourself first and make sure the atmosphere surrounding you is always peaceful. Type 9 always shows understanding for conflicting opinions. He measures all his behaviour by questioning what it contributes to the mood around him. That's the way to keep the peace. Type 9 people often lose their plans in the agendas of others and smoothly adapt to what is around them. Conversely, they have trouble setting priorities, deciding what needs to be done first and what later. After all, in order to set priorities you need to decide what is more important than something else. That's why type 9 is an master of procrastination. He doesn't act until deadlines loom, because a missed deadline is more of a disturbance than performing the task. That's the type of trigger that type 9 generally needs from the world to start acting.

***If you keep yourself satisfied, then things will remain peaceful and harmonious.***

Type 9 doesn't like to make distinctions, and doesn't enjoy distinguishing himself. Sometimes he demands so little attention that he almost becomes invisible. He avoids situations where he is called upon to pick sides. Type 9 hopes to circumvent having to show his true colours, so he can dampen any disturbance and keep the peace at all costs. He does have an opinion, but he would rather not openly share it. He knows the power of refusal very well: if you don't like something, just dig your heels in. He is a champion of passive resistance.

By nature, type 9 dislikes upheaval. People who speak too loudly, draw a lot of attention to themselves, stand out from the crowd, or who go after their passion guns blazing are often seen as intense and disruptive. Before you know it there can be a conflict. Conflict, to type 9, represents more than an argument or a fight. Every agitation, every instance of friction, everything that disturbs the peace feels like conflict to him.

***If there is a disturbance, then there is conflict.***

In order to avoid coming into conflict with the world around him, type 9 puts on an attitude of tolerance. He understands everything and everyone. Every statement has an essence of truth. In effect, he sedates all emotions inside and outside himself. Both the highest highs and the lowest lows are smoothly toned down. Nothing is particularly exciting or horrible. Nothing is important enough to get worked up about. Time heals all wounds. Let's sleep on it, let's smooth it over; everything will turn out just fine. Type 9 hopes to subdue all intense emotions; he is practically allergic to them. Before you know it, they lead to impulsive behaviour and overreactions, which can cause discord and ruin the ambience. By sedating his own emotions and subduing all primary reactions, type 9 tends to display mainly secondary behaviour. He is reactive and has a wait-and-see attitude, hoping to spark as little reaction as possible in the outside world.

***If you smooth over everything, making nothing significant, then you maintain the harmony and peace.***

Naturally, this strategy comes with a price. By smoothing over everything and subduing every conflict, you tend to create a lot more disquiet than you aim for. For example, one of my children's head teachers was a type 9 person. All complaints and disagreement from parents and teachers were expertly suppressed and dampened down. According to him it was never as bad as it seemed, nothing was a big deal, and everything would always turn out ok. It caused a lot of disruption, because people did not feel they were taken seriously and always felt like they had to be even clearer and more persistent in order to be heard. They weren't getting through to him, and so they tried even harder.

This illustrates how smoothing over things can cause more intensity in the long run. If you always work to keep the peace, you end up creating hostility. Before you know it, you end up in the middle of all that discord and conflict. That's exactly what type 9 wants to avoid. It's outside his comfort zone. When there is conflict, his unconscious coach springs into action to motivate him to do what he does best: protecting the ambience and restoring the peace, sedating and subduing intense emotions. This is his arena. All disruption and conflict are expertly avoided. It's the safest way to be. That's how type 9 unconsciously keeps his vicious cycle going, and how his unconscious coach works overtime to keep him in his comfort zone.

## Conclusion

Whichever your personality type, the pattern is the same: we want to be in our comfort zone. That's where we feel happy and safe. Because we can never get enough of it, we stay in our comfort zone so much we end up overdoing it, and paying for it. It's like a large, all-you-can-eat buffet: before you know it, you've put too much on your plate and eaten way more than is good for you. You get stomach problems, or gain unwanted weight. Similarly, a glass of wine can be harmless and enjoyable, but before you know it, you're having two or more. Two glasses of wine aren't as fulfilling as they used to be, so you have three instead. Without realising it you enter the danger zone.

To sum up, everything that feels comfortable makes you want to have more of it. Unfortunately, it isn't always wise to give in; this comes at a price. If you want to break out of a pattern in life, then you must first see what you are doing. Even more importantly, you must see why you do it. The answer to that question comes with discovering your unconscious motivation, with meeting your unconscious coach. Self-awareness is step 1; next up is step 2: stepping outside your comfort zone. That's what the final chapter is about. First, though, let's examine what happens during a professional coaching session without awareness of unconscious motivations.

# 4

# Coach alert: beware the unconscious coach!

Finding a good coach is no easy feat. Thankfully, the number of people who coach with awareness of unconscious motivations is increasing, as well as the number of people who attempt to find out your unconscious convictions before working with you. These coaches at least try to expose the way you interpret the world, and that's a great start. The moment we understand how much of what we do is unconsciously decided, we are well on our way towards good coaching. This idea isn't just something we came up with; it has been proven scientifically time and time again. In his book *The smart unconscious* for example, Dutch psychologist and scholar Ap Dijksterhuis explains how our unconscious determines everything. Our unconscious guides our behaviour, our thinking and our feelings with a processing capacity about 200,000 times greater than our conscious mind. Our conscious selves don't have much influence over our actions.

> Our unconscious coach (unconscious motivation) is many times more powerful than our conscious selves are.

Before you set out with your coach, therapist or trainer, here are a few handy pointers. If you see one of the following situations happening, we suggest it's time to question, if not change, your choice of coach.

1. When the coach mainly gives behavioural advice.
2. When the coach thinks you know yourself best.
3. When the coach is unaware of his own motivations.
4. When the coach is just applying techniques to you.
5. When the coach thinks you need to "think positively".

6. When the coach mainly works intuitively.
7. When the coach understands you.
8. When the coach thinks your circumstances are to blame.

## 1. WHEN THE COACH MAINLY GIVES BEHAVIOURAL ADVICE

Only recently I was enjoying an interesting TV show. One of the benefits of knowing about unconscious motivations is that all TV shows suddenly become interesting. Even when you are completely uninterested in the subject of the show, it can be good fun looking for people's motivations; it's interesting and addictive! Anyway, this show is called *Help, My husband has a hobby!* and focuses on people who are so engrossed in their hobbies that their relationship with their partner is in danger. The viewer was introduced to the wife in the story, who complained about her husband's hobby, and the husband who had no idea what to do with the complaints. Was he a callous jerk or just exhausted from all the criticism? The host, as well as the show's go-getting coach were in agreement: the husband was going to get it; the wife was a victim who badly needed their help. The wife's complaint was that her husband didn't make enough time for her and the family; he worked all day and spent the evenings at the computer. After about fifteen minutes I noticed that something about the lady in question triggered my annoyance no end, so my respect for the husband only increased. All he was really doing was sitting there on the couch every evening with his laptop. I would have made for the hills long before.

Ok, so he wasn't really present, but when you're constantly complained about you learn not to open your mouth, right? So I was on team husband; the host and coach were on team wife. That's how quickly these things happen. Fortunately we were both wrong.

These types of situations are always chicken-and-egg stories. What came first: the husband's behaviour or the wife's complaining? Whatever the answer, there is an interesting pattern now that calls for closer investigation. It's much more interesting to find out what both parties are contributing to this pattern, and which convictions are keeping it in place, than to try to put the blame on either person.

The coach was a practical, problem-solving woman, who I suspect is a type 3 person. She had a different approach in mind. The husband got a stern talking-to: “How could you neglect your wife like this?” and, “Do you even realise what you're doing?”

Then the children were interviewed, and, misty-eyed, told the host how much they missed their father too. These sorts of things draw the viewer further and further into the mother's camp. The solution was crystal-clear: the laptop had to go, and so did all the other computers in the house. Next came a scene where, I kid you not, the father and kids tossed the computers out of the window.

“Problem solved!” we are meant to think. Well, um, no. The final scene shows how the two have fared since: both are on the couch staring, straight ahead, at the television. One screen has been replaced by another and, still, there is no communication. Before you know it, there could be another problem: what happens if they each want to watch something different? The complaint, as always, isn't the problem.

You can watch people being helped on television every day. Overfull houses are cleaned out, marriages are fixed and plenty of boxing bags are punched. That's how we are supposed to learn to stand up for ourselves and to release our anger. Most of it, however well meant, is pretty cringe worthy.

Once you know a little bit about how people work, you'll start to see how these programmes usually help people out of the frying pan and into the fire. *Obese: a year to save my life*, for example, is a British TV show that helps people lose weight by exercising more and eating better. This is a beautiful goal, of course, but do they ever find out the reason these people were so unhealthily overweight in the first place? Do they ever look for the real problem behind the complaint? No!

They make an effort to, but most explanations do not make sense. They blame a deceased parent, or bullying in school, childhood neglect, being laid off from work or the end of a relationship, but those explanations are the kind our conscious mind makes up because we want to find a reason for our behaviour. It is natural to do so; it gives us something to hold onto, but if those reasons were the true cause, then everyone who was bullied in school would now be overweight, or have body issues. That's simply not true. Sure, those kinds of suffering could have played a part in creating or facilitating the situation as it is today, but they are never the cause. As we explained earlier in this book, your circumstances do not determine who you are, but your motivations do determine how you deal with those circumstances. That's where you'll find the answer. No well-meaning TV show host, no matter how charming and how to the point their questions are, is going to get this information; people simply do not consciously know the answer. If they did, they most likely wouldn't be in this situation. People will not know the reason why they behave the way they do until they understand their unconscious motivation. Your unconscious motivation decides everything, including your lifestyle and diet.

Only when you know your unconscious motivation, can you structurally change your view of yourself and the world. This is how you can change your future behaviour and diet. When you find and alter the limiting conviction that is responsible for obsessive behaviour, you can effect permanent change. As it is, the *Obese* candidates have the opportunity to lose a lot of weight in a short time with a lot of guidance; afterwards they will have to go it alone. The only way of doing that successfully is by solving something of the real problem behind the complaint. That's more healthy and satisfying than any meal!

To illustrate this, a lot of *Obese* candidates happen to have a type 8 motivation. This doesn't mean that all people who suffer from obesity are type 8 people, or that all people with a type 8 motivation are obese. This personality type is only one of nine motivations that can lead people to become overweight in a variety of ways. Type 8 people, however, need to be in touch with their strength all the time. They do this by collecting energy, as it were. Only when you feel strong and powerful are you capable of handling the world. That's one of the core convictions of this personality type. So when you don't feel up to scratch, weak or just down, the unconscious type 8 motivation will dictate that you fix that a.s.a.p. This motivation prompts you to avoid feeling vulnerable at all times, and what will give your energy and strength faster than food?

A habit is formed easily, and there is another unconscious advantage to having a certain body type: being physically big can have the psychological, as well as physical, function of building a wall around you. Additionally, being more unattractive in the traditional sense might also keep others away. That's how you may unconsciously protect yourself from too much closeness, making it increasingly difficult to let others in. If you are someone who prefers to decide everything himself, the way type 8 people do, then that may be a reassuring thought. It's how type 8 can confirm to himself that, in the end, he is on his own in life. Consciously, type 8 people want love, contact and intimacy just like everybody else, but the unconscious self is just a little bit stronger. There are a few limiting convictions in the way. It's important to find these and alter them. Otherwise the obesity patient will only run into his next problem: what do you do when you have a thin body when unconsciously, it fits your self-image better to be overweight?

This example shows how it might happen that your conscious self wants to be skinny, but your unconscious self benefits more from being overweight. If you really want to help the *Obese* candidates then you need to make sure they know their unconscious motivations. Otherwise they will be back to their old body shapes in no time at all.

## 2. WHEN THE COACH THINKS YOU KNOW YOURSELF BEST

In order to emphasise the equal relationship between coach and client, the word of choice these days is *coachee.* Coachee sounds more laid-back than client and if you remove the last two letters it says *coach.* Indeed, many coaches believe clients know themselves best, and that they are capable of solving their own issues, capable of coaching themselves. This type of coach sees himself as someone who holds a mirror up to the client, as it were. It's enough to follow and mirror the client, this coach thinks, because he knows himself best.

Unfortunately, reality couldn't be more different. People are full of blind spots; one of the most difficult things to do is to perceive yourself accurately. Most people even have trouble describing what's bothering them in the first place: something isn't right; this is not how they want to keep going. They feel life could be better somehow, but yeah... what is the real problem? Is it their relationship that isn't up to scratch? Is it their partner? Or is it an old trauma from the past, and maybe the partner is just a catalyst? That happens in a lot of relationships, by the way. Unresolved pain from the past is dumped onto the partner. Sometimes your partner is even similar enough to one of your parents to give you a chance to work through some things again. These things don't happen by chance.

Maybe it's work then: you've been in a rut for ages; your colleague gets in your way; your boss has an ego big enough to fill the whole department. Or maybe it's because you spend so little time on yourself these days; there has been no time to go to the gym or take a long walk. You've slowly gained some pounds over the years and none of your clothes really fit anymore; you don't feel at home in your own skin.

Could that be it: just a general dissatisfaction with yourself? But surely you don't go to see a coach for that? You go to the gym, or go on a diet. But really you don't have the energy even for that. And why is it that you take care of yourself so poorly in the first place? There must be a deeper reason for that. You start looking more like your mum every day, even though you were always bothered by her dishevelled appearance. Could it be that you are more like her than you thought? Perhaps it's time to find out, so let's go see a coach! It couldn't hurt to try right? Unfortunately though, it can.

"Come on," the coachee thinks, realising from her coach's expectant look that she is meant to say something. The silence is starting to become uncomfortable. She goes for the relationship: "My husband and I are in a rut," she says. "One way or another, we keep miscommunicating." The coach nods understandingly. The coachee continues, "He's busy at work, I'm busy at work. After work we are exhausted. It's like we're a retired couple, and we don't even have kids yet!"

"Would you like that? To have children?" The coachee is startled. Oh dear, that must be what this is about: a hidden longing for a child. Would that be it? She turns pale. She can't believe she hasn't thought of that before. Suddenly there are tears in her eyes. Wow, after only ten minutes this coach has found out where her pain came from. So that's the reason for everything. That's why she gained weight: she was preparing for pregnancy. That's why she was starting to look more and more like her mother: she wants to be a mother herself. The fact that she didn't feel like doing anything anymore: she must have been psychologically preparing for life in and around the house. It all seems so logical now, why didn't she think of this sooner?

When the coach puts you in charge and only follows your lead, in the best-case scenario you have a good conversation. Somebody will listen to you, and you take your time to organise your thoughts; that's usually good for something. However, this type of coaching remains risky. Before you know it you are going to work on a complaint, and if you are unlucky you end up working on the wrong one. It remains a scattergun approach where you need something more targeted.

## 3. WHEN THE COACH IS UNAWARE OF HIS OWN MOTIVATIONS

Perhaps the coach in the previous example has a longing for children of her own, making this a typical case of projection. Perhaps she recognised her own story in that of her coachee, a situation where she was in a rut herself, how she blamed everything on her partner and finally ended the relationship in anger. Maybe now, twenty years later, she still regrets it because she never ended up having children. In the meantime she learnt coaching and dedicated herself to helping young women. She mainly helps them prevent the mistakes she made in life. She is very involved with them and deeply caring, almost thinking of them as her own children. Of course, you end up making a connection after a while. The wall in her office is completely covered in birth announcements. She feels the greatest pride when she looks at the card in the middle of the wall: "Jet," it says, her name. It's from a couple she mentored for years. They nearly gave up on having a child at all, but her determination helped them decide for IVF treatment and now they have the most precious baby girl, named after her! That's what we do it for in life, a wall filled with happiness. It goes some way towards compensating her unfulfilled longing. Never having had a child leaves a hole which isn't easily filled, she knows that very well. That's why she does this work with so much conviction.

Unfortunately, most coaches do not provide an insight into your unconscious motivations. Worse still, most coaches don't even know what it is they are aiming for unconsciously. That causes a lot of trouble. There is no question most coaches have the very best of intentions. When I read online discussions about coaching on various forums almost everybody seems to work together very hard to search for the best way to coach their clients. Good intentions alone, however, do not solve problems.

A coach who is unaware of his own motivations cannot help but project his own worldview onto you. Before too long you'll end up working on the coach's problem instead of your own.

Imagine your coach is a type 3 person, someone who likes solutions over problems. One common notion of type 3 people is that emotions only cost time: they are convinced that they need to earn their right to exist by achieving a lot of goals. Doing things is good, because when you do things you get results. The more check marks you can make on your list, the better. That means emotions are obstacles on the way to your target. They're allowed, but let's above all get to a solution quickly so we can move on. It could very well be that this type of coach, who likes to keep up the pace, doesn't take you to the real cause of the pain and sends you on your way with practical solutions. You'll end up working on the complaint instead of the problem, so the coaching remains a scattergun approach.

## 4. WHEN THE COACH IS JUST APPLYING TECHNIQUES TO YOU

When the *coachee* comes home her husband asks about her new coach. "Well, what can I say? She thinks I'm ready to have children." "Right," her husband says, "let's go for it." Three kids later the woman meets with a coach again. This time she is a client, which sounds a bit better than coachee, at least. This coach knows what he's talking about; he's an expert trained in "voice dialogue". He wants to understand her better and begins a dialogue with the selves inside her. There turns out to be a whole bunch of them. The easy self says, "Why don't you just stay home with the kids, you can always work later." The demanding self says severely, "Come on, you're being silly; it isn't too difficult to combine kids and work." Then there is her erotic self who order her to invest more in her sex life. Meanwhile, the self who likes to procrastinate puts her at ease again and tells her not to set the bar so high. The internal dialogues make her dizzy. The coach explains that she's in charge of this motley crew. Well, that's a relief... She can decide how much space each self gets. They are all sub-personalities that try to grab control, to be in charge. "Think of them as parts of you that want attention," the coach explains patiently. He compares it to a stage play: "This is your theatre company, these are your actors and you get to decide which part they all play." Right. "Go home and write down what the most important selves are telling you; keep a journal."

"Oh my god," the self who likes freedom says, "homework! That's the last thing I want to do." The ambitious self immediately corrects her: "I thought you wanted progress! Well, you'll have to work for it." With a tired voice the polite self says goodbye to the coach; he promises he will take a close look inside this week, at all the selves. The compassionate self, seeing how hard the coach is working and feeling sorry for him, says unconvincingly that the session was a real eye opener. "You're such a liar," her honest self immediately corrects.

> Every technique can be useful, as long as you know your unconscious motivations. First, the correct diagnosis needs to be made.

A week later the client calls 25 hours in advance (otherwise the session is still billed) because she wasn't able to do her homework. She is embarrassed. Apparently this is how little will power she has. She is never going to amount to anything. All those expensive coaches, seminars and books, and still she keeps falling back into old patterns. A friend comforts her. The friend just finished writing her autobiography with another coach. "It's very interesting to do," her friend says. "It gives you a sort of overview; you start seeing patterns, things that keep coming back." "Yeah, I know what patterns are," our client answers wearily.

Voice dialogue is a beautiful method, but only as long as it's used at the right time for the right reason. That goes for every method. When you know someone's unconscious motivation, you see what the problem behind their complaint is. Actually, one of the ways of finding out an unconscious motivation is with voice dialogue, as long as you know what you're doing. The method must serve the problem and not the other way around, otherwise we're still just taking a scattergun approach!

## 5. WHEN THE COACH THINKS YOU NEED TO "THINK POSITIVELY"

Then there is the moment when you have tried lots of coaches, seminars and books, but it hasn't helped you much. You become a bit discouraged, you think you're never going to learn. If you realise that your glass tends to be more half empty than half full only a week after an expensive seminar about positive thinking, does that mean there is something wrong with you? No! The only thing wrong, is the exaggerated fixation with positive thinking. What's worse, people are being fooled. You can't learn to think positively in a few days if it's not in your nature. You shouldn't even want to.

> Your unconscious motivations determine whether you're a matcher or a mismatcher, whether you see the glass half full or half empty. You can only learn positive thinking when you adjust a conviction.

Of course it can be a good idea to learn new behaviour if you tend to always focus on the negative. Especially if that's something which bothers you. But first you need to learn why that's where your focus is drawn. You need to find out your unconscious motivation. Then you'll understand your psychological investment in focusing on what is missing or negative. You'll know how you benefit from thinking that way, and what price you would have to pay to stop doing this. Yes, there is always a price. We are attached to our habits, even when they have stopped working for us; we would rather do what we know, than venture into the unknown. Again, we do this unconsciously. Consciously, we want improvement.

Positive thinking is a difficult thing to learn for mismatchers, people who tend to see the glass half empty. They automatically register what is missing, what should have been better, and what could go wrong. Without thinking, this is the first thing they scan for; it's in their nature. If you are born a mismatcher (and yes you are just born that way, you either are or you aren't) then your autopilot will always drive you to look for what is missing. What do you mean positive thinking? That's a nice thought, but things go wrong that way, the mismatcher thinks. Dangerous! His autopilot does not accept alternative behaviour.

Being able to mismatch is an amazing quality, by the way, as long as you don't exaggerate it. But, as we can learn from Daniel Ofman and his Core Quadrant, that goes for every quality. Everything you put "too" in front of, will end up working against you. It's great to be caring, but being too caring can lead to being overly anxious. Being positive is lovely, but if you are too positive you become naïve.

So if you are born a matcher, a natural positive thinker, it might be clever to take a moment to think about what might go wrong. This might definitely be wiser than becoming even more positive. Conversely, it is good for a mismatcher to connect with what *is* there, rather than what isn't, for a change. Conclusion: like most seminars, a seminar about positive thinking is usually entertaining at best. It gives you energy, it inspires you, and there are always a few insights to take home, but eventually you leave empty-handed. People who are a tad gloomy by nature, will never keep up the positive thinking. People who are already born cheery don't learn anything new. And yes, it may also be damaging: another investment that doesn't work out in the long run. It demotivates people from making another move, and it's still a scattergun approach!

## 6. WHEN THE COACH MAINLY WORKS INTUITIVELY

Many coaches explain, "I work very intuitively, from feeling, because your instincts never betray you." Well, I have bad news: your feelings are a bad counsellor. Last night, for example, I felt a great need for chocolate. I also felt like sleeping with my new colleague and suddenly I felt I had to sell my house. I had gone out to eat in Amsterdam with a friend, you see, and I just felt that that was the place where I wanted to live.

Still buzzing on the chocolate I looked online for house prices, and sure, I found the apartment of my dreams. I made an offer immediately, because it just felt so good. I still need to sell the old place, but my intuition is telling me this is going to work. Yes, there are many houses for sale in the area, but this one just has something extra. I felt it immediately the first time I walked in the door. It's just the whole atmosphere of the place, hard to explain. It just feels like a warm bath. Others will feel it too. Anyway, in the meantime I have put my house on sale, because they accepted my offer! It only proves this was meant to be. Now I just need to figure out how I am going to afford two mortgages in the near future, but I'll work it out. That new colleague lives in Amsterdam as well, by the way. Exciting! Ok, so he's married, but I feel like his marriage isn't doing so well anyway. I should lose weight, though, before moving. I should eat less chocolate and exercise more, but not right now; I feel like now is not the time.

> Your feelings are unreliable; they can change from minute to minute, so coaching on intuition is a risky business.

You were just feeling so good and suddenly you get bad news. You get up enthusiastically but stub your toe. You feel like being close but your partner pushes you away. Our state of mind changes throughout the day. One moment we are on fire and the next we feel discouraged.

So beware the intuitive coach, who coaches based on feeling. Your coaching is dependent on his intuition (projection!). Let's hope the coach isn't having a bad day, and doesn't recognise too many of your problems in his own life. Before you know it, you're working on solving the coach's problems (again). I would run for the hills if my doctor said, "I mainly work on intuition. Your stomach pains indicate appendicitis; I can just feel it." Give me a sound physical, an ultrasound please, and then a proper diagnosis. Intuition is a nice addition, but not a basis for action.

Intuitive coaches often think that you, too, need to listen to your intuition. They think you need to give space to your feelings. But how do you do that? Most people find it incredibly difficult to recognise, let alone express, their feelings. For all kinds of reasons we prefer to stay away from them. We are very cunning in doing so. We are completely unused to accurately perceiving and vocalising our feelings, so the words we find for them seldom fit.

Of course there is nothing wrong with letting your feelings inform you during the making of decisions; that's probably wise. Coaching on intuition alone, however, is nonsense. You need to keep your head straight as well, otherwise you end up doing more harm than good.

---

## 7. WHEN THE COACH UNDERSTANDS YOU

As a coach it happens before you know it. It's easy to go along with the client's complaint, to consider is as truth and forget that it's only your client's interpretation of the world. You need to remember that the client is only describing his subjective reality, and that as a coach you are always working with your client's subjective experience. His convictions and assumptions are interesting because they give information about his worldview.

> Dealing with the content of a complaint is one of the biggest pitfalls in coaching.

Unfortunately, many coaches tend to be distracted by the content of the story. It makes sense, right? That the client feels cheated? Wouldn't your world collapse if it happened to you? His wife cheated on him with the neighbour. Meanwhile, the client seems to be a solid fellow, a good guy. He is a tall, broken, man, a gentle giant, talking about the demise of his marriage with tears in his eyes. He talks about his wife with so much love; where can you find a man like that these days?

Before you know it, you go along happily with your client's complaint.

You understand the client's frustration, and that's where it happens; you are part of his pattern. Just wait until you speak with his wife; her interpretation of things is probably entirely different. During the next session she explains to you that the dear man has cheated on her time after time. She speaks of him going on business trips, letting it all hang out, and that she has been feeling neglected for years. Sure, he brings her beautiful gifts; she isn't missing out on a material level.

He even built an amazing house for her. However, she started to feel more and more that she was living in a sort of golden cage. She felt more like his property than his partner.

The man, who first seemed a quintessential good guy, now appears to have an aggressive streak as well. "Woman, stop whining; you have everything you could ever want. Those little adventures mean nothing; you know that. But you got it into your head to start an actual relationship. With the neighbour of all people! You're just a spoilt little girl, untrustworthy!

Now the wife explains her experience of things. She was always alone in that huge house. Its maintenance was so much work that she rarely left home. And then there was the neighbour, a nice man, who lives alone. He spent most of his days at home writing. They get to talking; it's innocent at first, but one thing leads to another. She's ashamed of herself; this behaviour doesn't fit her self-image at all. Cheating is a horrible thing but she fell in love with this man, and he with her. Now she doesn't know what to do anymore.

"Why don't you just take him?" the man spews. "If you'd rather date some poor idiot than live a decent life, then just leave!" He is in a rage. His ego is bruised. He gave her everything. Unfortunately though, love is not for sale.

Yes, nothing is what it seems. So as a coach you must beware before you connect with the content of a story. You mustn't feel too understanding, because before you know it you will choose sides. That's not your job. A coach is not a judge.

Of course, every coach is fooled once in a while, but this is something to heed carefully. Empathy is good, and every client is free to experience what he wants. However, it is not a coach's task to understand the client. A coach must help his client understand himself. Most importantly, the client must understand how he interprets things, and what his limiting convictions are. These keep the problem alive.

---

## 8. WHEN THE COACH THINKS THE CIRCUMSTANCES ARE TO BLAME

This is a classic mistake. Everybody does this, all the time. Psychologist or not, we keep on looking for explanations. It comforts us. As long as we have an explanation, as long as we think one thing is caused by another, we feel we have some control. Of course the kid next door smokes pot; wouldn't you, if your father were unemployed and your mother walking around so unkempt? At least we do things differently. At least we're involved parents and we're setting the right example.

Until the day your child comes home stoned, and he turns out to smoke pot regularly himself. That means it's time to adjust your view of things. Painful, but things just aren't that simple. Life isn't logical and fair. Good parents will have bratty children and children from the most broken families will turn out really well.

Of course, parenting is good for something; there is a great deal you can teach and provide for your children. I personally believe strongly that a properly packed rucksack can make your life a whole lot more pleasant. Parents can shape and correct. They can be present and supportive. But your child's blueprint has already been determined.

> The way we assign meaning is born from our unconscious motivation, our psychological DNA, and is not determined by our circumstances.

That's why it's best to quickly discover your child's motivation. Then you will understand what drives him and how you can best guide him. You will see what he needs to learn and what his pitfalls are. Then you can draw much more accurate conclusions, especially if you are aware of your own motivations as well. This way you prevent yourself from projecting your convictions onto your child. It's the cleanest, most efficient way!

It could be, for example, that your son is doing drugs because he wants to feel connected with his friends, who all do it too. He turns out to be a type 6 person who above all wants to be loyal to others. He actually doesn't care much for weed, but he joins in nevertheless because he wants to fit in instead of stand out. Perhaps his challenge is to learn to be more conspicuous. Perhaps the smoking will stop on its own. That's better than just solving the complaint, the weed smoking. If you focus on that, then he will do something else to fit in next time; you will not have solved the real problem. When he learns to stand out more, however, he will benefit from that in other areas as well. That's how you solve multiple complaints at once, because you deal with the real problem.

Long story short, we draw conclusions based on a cause and effect that do not make sense. That's one of the biggest coaching pitfalls. It's because of his childhood, his freckles or his weight; it's because his father used to hit him or because his mother spoilt him. Yes, these things may have played a part, but there is something stronger than all that: your unconscious motivation. Neither your childhood nor your circumstances determine your behaviour. The way you assign meaning to them will always be the deciding factor.

The other day, in a tear-jerker TV show, I heard someone say, "Because he was sick for so long, he has lost all faith in life." Nonsense. A friend of mine who was seriously ill for a long time makes every day into a holiday now that she is better. Because she was sick for so long! It's not our circumstances that determine who we are; it's our unconscious motivation that determines how we deal with those circumstances. A coach who understands that can help you deal with the situation differently and learn something to make life easier.

## IT CAN HURT TO TRY

Oh well, it can't hurt to try! We say enthusiastically when a friend tells us he is going in for a round of coaching or therapy. Unfortunately, this isn't true. Most people who see a coach who is unaware of his own motivations will end up leaping out of the frying pan and into the fire. This danger exists with every coach who doesn't know his own motivations or doesn't see through behaviour to the underlying motivations. It's like a crash diet: it might seem to help for a while, but afterwards we gain weight twice as fast. The explanation is simple: your body recognises the extreme diet as starvation and goes into survival mode, holding onto every calorie for dear life. There need to be reserves! The effect: most people gain weight faster after a diet. In fact, many people who diet often and strictly end up only gaining weight in the long run.

It works the same way with coaching. Often it's nothing more than fighting symptoms without knowing the disease. The complaint is solved but the problem isn't. The client feels good for a minute. He has received a few tips for a better life, holds on to these for a month, and then slips back just as easily into the old pattern. He is more frustrated than ever, because if coaching doesn't work then how is he supposed to solve his problem? It's discouraging!

Because your unconscious self is stronger than your conscious self, most coaching only offers temporary relief. Your conscious self wants change; your unconscious self resists for all it's worth. So behavioural advice only has limited functionality. No matter how good the advice is, no matter how much the coach wants to help you, without proper knowledge of unconscious motivations, coaching remains a Sisyphean task. Your unconscious coach will force you back to your old behaviour in no time. Only when your coach addresses your unconscious coach, when he understands what your unconscious coach is striving for, will the coaching process lead to something. In order to do so, however, the coach first needs to become conscious.

# 5 Step out of your comfort zone!

## More of the same

People often go to see a coach so they can learn more of the same. They go to learn more of what they already know so they can stay in their comfort zone. They do this unconsciously, because, as noted earlier, consciously we often really do want improvement. It happens without our realising. Your unconscious coach makes sure of that. He wants you to keep doing what you're used to doing. Type 9 will try another course in conflict avoidance, to deal with the disquiet and friction even better. Meanwhile, type 5 will take another time management course, so he can plan his time and energy even more prudently. Type 4 will follow the workshop "finding your true self", having just finished a course in intuitive living. Next year he wants to spend a week in silence in Bali, to make even more contact with his deepest feelings. Type 3's battle plan involves all kinds of courses and training; you never know when one might come in handy! Type 2, unfortunately, does not have the time for coaching and courses; he's way too busy making a difference to others. He needs to stay available to the people around him. Type 1 travelled to New York, to see the international specialist in organisation and structuring. Type 1 wants to be even better at that. Loyal type 6 learns to be a better team player in a group weekend in the woods. He will be even better at anticipating the expectations of others. Type 8 does an online course called "Find your strength!" It's great to be able to do that in your own time, in your own way. A real challenge for type 8... Not!

It might be satisfying for a minute, because it's right up your alley, but it rarely makes you wiser. That's because it's more of the same, more of your comfort zone. The trouble is that it often feels so good, because it's so familiar to you. That's the same as confirming your convictions. It feels comfortable. It's why we often keep learning more of the same, in order to stay in our comfort zone.

> We like to learn things that confirm our convictions. That feels good; apparently our worldview was correct!

"Optimists live longer" is what type 7 filters from a seminar about positive thinking. It's a huge relief, because this once again confirms his unconscious conviction. Optimism is his middle name, so this feels good. Every time he feels down, when things are bad, he tells himself to stay optimistic. Except, one day this doesn't work anymore. He feels depressed. Well, that's what happens when you systematically repress your negative feelings. In time you pay the price. So type 7 goes to see a coach: "Help, I am feeling down. Whatever I do, nothing is fun anymore." Before you know it, the coach will advise him to go out and do more things that bring him joy. Great plan, type 7 thinks, I'm not going to limit myself anymore. You only live once. My coach is the best, type 7 thinks, he totally understands me. By that he means, "Yay, I get to stay in my comfort zone!"

> People often want more of the same, more of their comfort zone, so nothing changes.

Let's be clear that we all go to see a coach with the best of intentions. When people are tired of the way their lives are playing out, they really do want to change. And most coaches keep informing themselves with new courses and training to help people with their transformations. They are truly motivated to make a difference. Everybody does their best, that's not the problem. But good intentions don't cause lasting change; you are going to need more for that.

## The key to happiness

If you learn more of the same, you'll keep doing the same. If you want to break through a pattern, you must do what you're unaccustomed to doing. In other words, you need to take a step, or place a toe, outside your comfort zone.

This is easier said than done. How do you even do that? The answer is simple: by allowing something into your life you would usually avoid. That can be pretty frightening, of course: you've just spent your whole life staying away from it. You truly think that allowing this thing in can be life threatening. That's why your unconscious coach does whatever he can to make sure you stay in your comfort zone. It's why you systematically avoid certain behaviours, because they are a contradiction of your favourite way of survival, so it feels unsafe. That's the reason we unconsciously fight change with all we have. We want to grow, but we don't want to experience growing pains.

> In order to step outside your comfort zone you need to do something you've been avoiding up to now.

## Your unconscious coach is working overtime.

Your unconscious coach needs to work really hard in order to keep you inside your comfort zone, and to stop you from doing anything that doesn't fit your ideal image. You need to stay away from something; something needs to be avoided. That takes a lot of energy. The drama is that you can't win. Because we are so extremely attached to our comfort zone; because we want so much of it, we end up exactly where we don't want to be.

Type 1 sets the bar so high (comfort zone) that he can never meet it, causing him to continually feel his imperfection. He ends up being in contact with the exact thing he wants to stay away from. Type 2 wants to be needed by others so much, that he continually overreaches himself and ends up needing others instead. That's exactly the thing he despises most. Whatever your motivation, everybody does the same thing. Everybody unconsciously works towards the thing he or she is trying to avoid. This is explained in more detail under principle 5.

What is the solution to all this business? To recognise and admit that you are imperfect and needy, that we all fail in life, that you are mediocre and dependent and insecure. The key is to accept that life hurts, that you are vulnerable and that conflict is a part of life too. If you can manage to do that, you can stop fighting reality: you can relax, because every part of your human experience is acceptable, everything is allowed to be there. In fact, everything *is* there and was all along. When we accept that, our lives will be more balanced. That's good, because we save ourselves lots of frustration and energy.

## Accepting reality: adjusting an ideal image

We feel frustrated when our ideal image doesn't match up with reality. Instead of accepting reality we set the bar even higher. We want it our way no matter what, otherwise we feel threatened. Even though in the end it's much more threatening to deny reality as it is. After all, that's hard work that will eventually exhaust us. No one has ever burnt out from hard work; many have burnt out from the way they work. Often this involves a resistance of reality. Things should be better, more loving, faster, more real, more objective, more together, more fun, stronger, or more relaxed. Things should be different from how they are. It's a fight you cannot win, because you can only change reality so much.

> It is usually wiser to adjust your ideal image than to change reality, but in order to do so you must first know what that ideal image is.

This book explains how we are always chasing after an ideal image that often differs from reality. Instead of accepting reality we try to protect and defend ourselves with all we have. That's how our defence mechanisms are born. Restraint, suppression, identification, distinction, withdrawal, projection, rationalisation, denial and sedation, these are the defence mechanisms of the nine personality types in a row.

It already gives us a certain peace to understand that we are fighting an aspect of life that we have trouble dealing with. If you can see this, you realise that the ideal image you are chasing is unattainable. That means you can see how it is smarter to adjust the ideal image a little bit, without becoming despondent. That's the other extreme, and despondency leads us nowhere. The challenge is realism. The challenge is to learn to accept life the way it is, with all its sunny sides and its dark sides. That gives peace and balance. When you stop avoiding, you will free up energy, acceptance and connection. Then you can start living, instead of surviving.

## The exhausted coach

Most coaches work way too hard, and often do not get proper results. That's too bad for the client, but also for the coach. It happens because the most important thing is forgotten: mapping the unconscious motivations.

That's a missed opportunity, because a coach who knows his client's motivations, learns a lot about the way that client assigns meaning to his experiences. That coach understands his client's world. He understands which convictions the client lives by and what that person wants to avoid. That's the root of all his client's problems, and knowing the root of someone's problems is handy if your business is to help solve them.

> Most coaches work with the content of their clients' stories, but that's pointless, complicated and exhausting.

A coach that does not know his client's motivations can only ever work with the content of his story. If you work that way, then every word should matter equally. This coach needs to listen well, because he needs to catch and remember everything his client says. Before he knows it, he is keeping huge files and records for every client. What does he gain from this? Nothing. It only costs him a lot of time and effort. People have the tendency to speak in catchall phrases. This means that in the best case scenario the report of a session looks like several pages of these kinds of phrases. It becomes even worse when one unconscious coach reports to another. During a peer meeting, for example, coach A explains to peer B, "This client easily feels rejected. It's because of his childhood, his mother never had time for him. He now has an inferiority complex, which is why he always goes for the wrong kind of woman. They end up rejecting him as well. That's why I'm teaching him to become more resilient, to trust in himself more." What does coach B now know? Nothing.

It's unclear what coach A means by rejection. Funny conclusions are made: when your mother doesn't have time for you, you develop an inferiority complex?! That doesn't sound logical, and it says more about the convictions of coach A than about reality. What does he mean when he says the client needs to become more resilient? Does he need to go to the gym more often? Does he need to build a large wall around his house? How do you do that? And how do you trust in yourself more?

Of course, coach B also projects his convictions onto this story. He has yet another different understanding of rejection, inferiority complex, the wrong women, and so on. That makes this conversation useless at best. It might appear to be helpful, and the intentions behind it are good, but I doubt whether it will help the client. Most likely, it would be much more beneficial to the client if he understood that he was a type 4 person. He would then learn to see how he causes his own rejection, because has the conviction that he is less worthwhile than others. That's just how he is put together. By nature he compares himself negatively to others; he rejects himself. His mother couldn't really have helped that. Perhaps she could have encouraged him to love himself, she could have been home more often and given him more attention. But even then there's no way of knowing if it would have made a difference. Type 4's own unconscious coach is attached to rejection.

It could also be the case, however, that the coach is a type 4 person herself. It could be that the client never even used the word rejection. That he was talking about insecurity or a fear of failure. Perhaps he was bothered by his mother's absence and perhaps she only criticised him when she was home. Perhaps her criticism bothered him more than her absence, but the coach filtered out the former because in his view the latter is the root of all misery in the world: that fits his worldview and so that's what he heard.

**In order to coach people with a clear vision, a coach needs to become aware of his own unconscious motivations. Otherwise he will project.**

In short, many coaches interpret all they can. They fill in the blanks and assign meaning based on a collection of catchall phrases. They do this without thoroughly questioning words and assumptions and without knowing what really motivates the client.

A coach who knows how he works and what motivates him, on the other hand, also knows which lens he uses to see the world. This coach knows how he colours things, how he assigns meaning to things. He will work more accurately, because there is less projection. That's because this coach understands what belongs to him, and what belongs to the other person in a conversation. Above all, a conscious coach avoids trying to find the cause of problems in the outside world. He doesn't draw strange conclusions of cause and effect. Those kinds of conclusions are usually subjective and coloured and give anything but a clear picture of reality.

## What does a motivation-conscious coach do?

When people come to see a coach, they often have a complaint. I am bothered by procrastination, is one such complaint. A motivation-conscious coach knows that there are nine variations on this theme, one for every personality type. Type 1, for example, might be bothered by procrastination because he will not start until everything is just right and according to his standards. Type 2 might be bothered by procrastination because he keeps focusing his attentions on others, leaving little time for his own things. Type 3 would prefer to postpone everything that doesn't lead to immediate success. A type 4 will procrastinate out of fear of rejection when he truly commits to something. Type 5 postpones for as long as he doesn't have a hundred percent of the information and type six does this as longs as he is in doubt and unsure of expectations. A type 7 person may procrastinate when he needs to do something annoying, just because he prefers having fun, and a type 8 may postpone the things that don't give him enough energy. Procrastination is easy for type 9, because he doesn't really consider anything particularly important. This makes it hard to set priorities and to get down to action. One complaint, nine variations.

The complaint is not the problem.

Imagine that the coach is seduced into trying to solve the complaint. He explains to type 2 that he needs to take more time for himself. That's great advice, but type 2 can't do anything with it. His unconscious self gets in the way. The coach may invite type 6 to create more clarity, and to trust in himself more, but this isn't going to work either. It's a shame, because it is potentially part of the solution for him. It doesn't work because more is needed: insight into the limiting conviction that keeps the problem in place. Whoever has insight into his limiting convictions can adjust them! That does help.

As I have stated earlier, a conscious coach will always look for the problem behind the complaint. Behind the complaint lies the conviction, which comes directly from the unconscious motivation.

**The complaint is not the problem**

Holding on and thoroughly questioning the complaint gets you to the real problem, and to the conviction and motivation behind it.

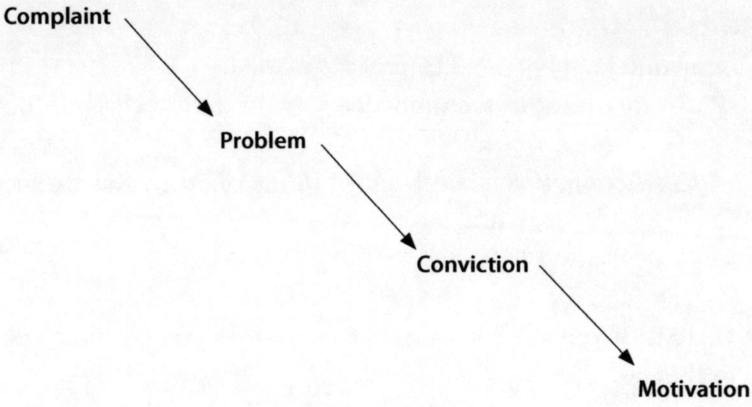


## One complaint, nine variations!

VARIATION 1

**Complaint:** I am bothered by procrastination.

**Problem:** It doesn't meet my standards.

**Conviction:** If you start something, then it must meet your standards.

**Motivation:** Type 1.

**ADJUSTED:** It's also ok to lower the bar.

VARIATION 2

**Complaint:** I am bothered by procrastination.

**Problem:** I need to be available to others.

**Conviction:** If you think of your own needs, then you are selfish.

**Motivation:** Type 2.

**ADJUSTED:** If you think of yourself first, you can be more help to others.

VARIATION 3

**Complaint:** I am bothered by procrastination.

**Problem:** I want to see immediate results and to check things off.

**Conviction:** If you check lots of things off, then you are successful.

**Motivation:** Type 3.

**ADJUSTED:** If you aim for long term goals, then you get more success in the end.

VARIATION 4

**Complaint:** I am bothered by procrastination.

**Problem:** I'm scared of connecting with others.

**Conviction:** If you connect with someone or something, then you will be rejected.

**Motivation:** Type 4.

**ADJUSTED:** If you connect with others, then you receive appreciation.

VARIATION 5

**Complaint:** I am bothered by procrastination.

**Problem:** I do not have all the information yet.

**Conviction:** If you are complete, then you are objective and independent.

**Motivation:** Type 5.

**ADJUSTED:** If you trust your feelings, then things will also turn out fine.

VARIATION 6

**Complaint:** I am bothered by procrastination.

**Problem:** I'm not sure what the expectations are and I'm still doubting.

**Conviction:** If you trust in others, then things will turn out ok.

**Motivation:** Type 6

ADJUSTED: If you trust in yourself, then things will turn out ok.

VARIATION 7

**Complaint:** I am bothered by procrastination.

**Problem:** I want to experience a lot and not be limited.

**Conviction:** If do a lot of fun things, then that brings you pleasure.

**Motivation:** Type 7.

ADJUSTED: If you focus your attention, then that brings you pleasure.

VARIATION 8

**Complaint:** I am bothered by procrastination.

**Problem:** It doesn't give me positive energy.

**Conviction:** If you are feeling good, then you can be strong.

**Motivation:** Type 8.

ADJUSTED: If you allow negative emotions to exist, then you can be strong.

**VARIATION 9**

**Complaint:** I am bothered by procrastination.

**Problem:** I find it difficult to treat something as important.

**Conviction:** If you stand out, then you will create friction in the world around you.

**Motivation:** Type 9.

**ADJUSTED:** If you treat yourself as important, then you will create peace inside yourself.

> If you work with the CPCM model, you'll solve the real problem.

One complaint, nine problems, nine convictions and nine motivations (CPCM). If you follow this system, you will have a clear, and in a certain sense, logical approach. This way of working pays off, whether you want to find out for yourself what it is that is really bothering you, or you want to help someone else. It also works really well if you need to know why you haven't been feeling like your usual self lately, or if you are ready to make lasting changes in your life. In both cases the CPCM model will help you identify what is truly holding you back. It provides structure and keeps you sharp. It also prevents you from working on the level of the complaint, and so it prevents you from the dangers of only fighting symptoms. The model is simple and it forces you to look for the real problem behind the complaint. Behind this problem is a limiting conviction that is born from your unconscious motivation. That limiting conviction is what stands in the way of your solving your problem. Adjusting this conviction leads to the solution of the problem. On top of this, if you're lucky, you'll solve many complaints at once.

If type 9, for example, learns to take himself a tad more seriously, and to stand out more, many areas of his life will improve. If type 8 learns that negative emotions have an influence as well, that they don't necessarily make you vulnerable and that they even make you stronger in the long run, he will reap tremendous benefits. That's the power of adjusting convictions. You break through a pattern and solve many issues at once.

## TEN BENEFITS OF MOTIVATION CONSCIOUS COACHING

It will always be a challenge to coach "cleanly", without muddying the waters with projection and content. Whether you want to coach yourself or someone else, always keep the five principles in mind. If you understand these, you understand everything about how people work.

**The five principles**

1. Our unconscious systems motivate us 24/7
2. The complaint is not the problem
3. Behind every problem there is a conviction
4. The adjustment of a conviction leads to lasting change
5. There are nine unconscious motivations

Knowledge of your own motivations is immensely valuable. Whether you are coaching yourself of someone else, this knowledge has myriad benefits.

1 *You are working on a problem instead of a complaint.* When you look for the unconscious motivations behind a complaint, you will find the real problem. Then you will solve an issue at its core and break through a pattern.

2 *You will get to know your own filters and projections.* Your motivation shows you the lens through which you see yourself and the world. It determines how you interpret things and what you filter out from your experiences. If you know your own filter, you will understand why you think and act the way you do. This is also the way to avoid projecting your worldview on someone else. This will save you a lot of miscommunication.

3 *Your motivations do not change.* Motivations are more than just behaviour, and, above all, they are the same regardless of context. Your motivations are active 24/7, so you can stick with the here and now when you're trying to solve problems; there is no need to dig deep into someone's past. What a client does during a coaching session, he does at home and at work. It's in his psychological DNA, a blueprint of his personality. You might behave differently at work from the way you do at home, but your motivations stay the same. That's what makes motivation-conscious coaching such a sound method. It isn't bound to a certain context. Motivations are more than behaviour.

4 *When you solve a problem, you break through a pattern and solve many complaints at once.* That's what makes motivation-conscious coaching so effective in comparison with behavioural coaching. Often the latter type of coaching involves fighting symptoms, and it only solves a complaint, if it achieves anything at all. If you coach based on people's motivations, then you deal with a problem at its core. That's because when you adjust a conviction, you alter your vision of yourself and the world forever.

5 *Motivation-conscious coaching is simple and efficient.* It prevents the coach from coaching based on the content of a client's story, and having to make huge, extensive, reports. It also prevents him from having to figure everything out from scratch with every new client. Never again does he have to make complicated and convoluted analyses in order to understand the client's problem. If you know someone's motivations, then you understand how he has created his problems. You will see how every complaint is a variation on this theme. Every person wants to avoid something with all their might, and that's where their problems come from.

6 *Motivation-conscious coaching is assessable.* Whether you are coaching yourself or someone else, check whether you have adjusted a limiting conviction and if the alternative allows for some-

thing previously avoided. That's the way to measure successful coaching.

7 *An insight into motivations has lasting benefits.* The moment you know your unconscious motivations, you will see what it is you do, and most importantly why you do it. That knowledge only deepens. If you receive an insight into your motivations you will continually learn to understand yourself better over time. That knowledge allows you to be the best coach you can be, for yourself as well as others.

8 *People with self-awareness are more fun.* People with self-knowledge are good company, for themselves and for others. That's because their self-image is correct and they do not profess nonsensical things about themselves. They know what drives them, and that's why you can confront them about their actions. They are open to feedback, which makes life easier for others.

9 *When you know your motivations, you know what belongs to you and what belongs to the other person in interactions.* That's handy, because we tend to put our own issues on other people's plates. We feel uncomfortable, incapable or frustrated and are inclined to think those feelings are caused by those around us. When you understand how you work, you will see how you cause most of your own frustrations. That prevents you from blaming others for your troubles.

10 *An insight into your motivations and those of others makes you accepting of yourself and others.* When we understand that everyone has their own preferred strategy and is driven by an unconscious motivation, and that we all see the world differently, that increases mutual understanding. That understanding means we do not judge each other so harshly. This is how motivation-conscious coaching makes the world a better place!

# 6
# Becoming conscious of your unconscious coach

This book has explained in five principles the importance of an understanding of unconscious motivations if you truly want to make a difference. It is essential information, whether you want to improve your own life or coach someone in improving theirs. This information is crucial because you are driven 24/7 by your unconscious motivation, the unconscious coach that tries to keep you in your comfort zone at all times. No amount of will power or perseverance can fight that. No matter how much you want to change something about yourself or your life, your unconscious self will sabotage any and all change. All your unconscious coach wants to do is to convince you that your old behaviour is better, safer and more efficient. After all, you will always make your unconscious convictions come true. So if you are convinced that you need to accomplish a lot in life, like type 3, then it's in your best interest to keep up a speedy pace. After all, the faster you go, the more you can do. Your conscious self, after your second burnout, might think of slowing down a bit. However, your unconscious coach will make sure you get back to normal as soon as possible, back to your comfort zone. Your unconscious coach will try to convince you otherwise as fast as he can; after all, you stand to gain a lot from your high pace: it's how you earn your right to exist. You don't just give up on that; your unconscious coach will make sure of it.

The coach or psychologist you end up with, as a type 3 person, after your burnout, the one who advises you to slow down, is probably right. The problem is that you will never keep it up unless you understand why you were running so fast in the first place. You will never learn to slow your pace unless you can see where the urge to achieve comes from. You must identify your psychological interest in doing this. You do have an interest in it; otherwise you wouldn't have made achieving goals your highest purpose in life. If you want to understand why you do what you do, it's essential to realise which convictions lie behind your behaviour. Then you can make a cost-benefit analysis. How does this behaviour benefit me and what does it cost me? If you realise it costs more than you gain from it, it's time to adjust a conviction. That will always mean allowing for something you have been avoiding in life.

If you keep a fast pace in life, then you can achieve a lot; that's one conviction of type 3 people. When you realise, however, that this might one day be your undoing (that it might eventually cause a burnout or heart attack) then perhaps you will be willing to adjust that conviction. In that case, it could just so happen that you realise you can accomplish a lot more when you slow down a bit. After all, you will probably live longer, make fewer mistakes that need to be rectified, and you might even end up enjoying what you are doing a whole lot more. That means it's a good idea for type 3 to live by the following alternative conviction instead: when you slow down, you can achieve more. Of course, this might be something of a shake-up to a type 3's worldview. "Who will I be if I achieve less?" type 3 thinks. To him, it feels like failure. Still, that adjusted conviction will be his key to lasting success.

When you understand your motivation, you will know which convictions your unconscious coach wants you to live by. This process of self-awareness will allow you to adjust the convictions that do more harm than good, and to replace them with alternative ones. This will change your vision of yourself and the world. The moment you change a conviction because the old one is obsolete, there is no way back. It changes your worldview forever, so that you live more and more in accordance with your new conviction.

## LIVE THE BEST LIFE YOU CAN!

Hopefully the moral of this story is clear: if you dare to integrate something you naturally avoid into your life, then this will bring you great comfort in the end. It will extend your comfort zone.

That's why it's so essential to understand which comfort zone you are attached to in the first place. Only then can you see what you are unconsciously striving for and avoiding in life, only then can you make the choice to step out of that comfort zone. That's when you will see how you have the tendency to turn your comfort zone into your own prison. Fortunately, you will also have the key to escape from that prison of your own making.

It will feel good, because everything you are bothered by in life, whether it's in your own behaviour or someone else's, will be much easier to place. After all, everything we know comes from the way we interpret things, our unconscious motivation. Similarly, learning to see the world and ourselves differently can solve nearly all our frustrations. When we adjust our ideal image and become more realistic we end up making our lives more fun. That's because we can stop putting our energy towards avoiding something that can't be avoided. After all, there are risks in life: we can fall ill, have bad luck, suffer hard knocks or even be injured by others. We will certainly die, but in the meantime we are sometimes painfully ignored, unseen, underestimated and humiliated. We regularly fail and deal with rejection and pain. People abuse and even violate us; and we do the same to them and ourselves. We do all this because we are only human, and because most of what we do is done unconsciously. Our intentions aren't to blame. It is our lack of self-insight that breaks us and makes life unnecessarily complicated.

When you get to know your unconscious motivation, then you will see how you defend your comfort zone with everything you've got. You will also see how that often ends up damaging you, and others. You will see how we all put up walls to make sure nobody messes with our comfortable little life. But is it really that comfortable? Or is it mostly safe and familiar and is that why it seems comfortable?

Are you really living your life, or is it more like surviving? It's worthwhile investigating that, and becoming conscious of what you're unconsciously doing. At the very least you will understand why you are doing it. That will give you a chance to break out of negative patterns forever! Insight leads to perspective!

It makes you more human, which is great for you and others. Discover your unconscious motivations, step out of your comfort zone and live the best life you can!

Colofon



Cover design: Riesenkind
Author photo: www.hadewychveys.nl
Lay-out: V3-Services
Printing: Ten Brink

First published March 2015

ISBN 978 94 6309 000 1
E-ISBN 978 94 6309 999 8
NUR 770



The Dutch Library

Marmer Publishers
De Botter 1
3742 GA BAARN
T: +31 649881429
I: www.uitgeverijmarmer.nl
E: info@uitgeverijmarmer.nl

www.vcirkelacademie.nl